SARGONIC TEXTS
IN THE LOUVRE MUSEUM

MATERIALS FOR THE ASSYRIAN DICTIONARY
NO. 4

SARGONIC TEXTS
IN THE LOUVRE MUSEUM

by

I. J. GELB

THE UNIVERSITY OF CHICAGO PRESS

CHICAGO, ILLINOIS

Library of Congress Catalog Card Number: 75–111600

THE UNIVERSITY OF CHICAGO PRESS, CHICAGO 60637
The University of Chicago Press, Ltd., London, W.C. 1

PHOTOLITHOPRINTED BY CUSHING - MALLOY, INC.
ANN ARBOR, MICHIGAN, UNITED STATES OF AMERICA
1970

TABLE OF CONTENTS

PREFACE

General Remarks

This volume contains all the unpublished
Sargonic material in the Louvre Museum, with the
exception of the Sargonic texts derived from the
excavations of Lagash and Susa.

The texts were transliterated by me mainly in
the summers of 1950 and 1960. I had occasion to
collate some difficult readings in 1965 and 1966.

Of the one hundred and seventy texts here published, fifty-eight texts are reproduced in photographs in the twenty-five plates at the end of the
volume. Because of their importance, all the twenty-
one witnessed texts, mainly purchase contracts, are
given in photographic reproduction; for other groups
and sub-groups of texts selected specimens are offered
to enable scholars to get the feel of the schools of
writing in different areas and periods. The tablets
are reproduced in their original size.

The great majority of the Akkadian lexical and
grammatical items found in the texts of this volume
have been utilized in the past editions of my MAD II
and III under the Louvre AO entries. The additional
items have been entered in the new editions of MAD II
and III, which are being prepared for publication.

All the citations and crossreferences in this
volume, especially in the Indices, are by the Louvre
AO numbers, not by numbers of texts in this volume.

This was done in order to facilitate the finding of corresponding occurrences in the MAD II and III volumes. Citing by the AO numbers should cause no difficulties since the sequence of the texts in this volume corresponds rigidly to the sequence of the AO numbers.

I wish to express my heartfelt gratitude to Messrs. Jean Nougayrol, André Parrot, and Pierre Amiet for placing the texts at my disposal and generally for making my work in the Louvre both pleasant and profitable. I am grateful also to Mr. Maurice Lambert for collating several difficult occurrences in 1965, and to Mr. Miguel Civil for contributing a number of valid suggestions in the interpretation of the texts. I am happy to acknowledge Mr. Lambert's help in supervising the production of the photographs.

Provenience and Date of Tablets

All the texts in this volume have been acquired piecemeal through the years by the Louvre Museum; none come from controlled excavations.

All the known information about the accession of the texts, as noted at the beginning of each text in this volume, was copied from the Louvre catalogues.

With the exception of texts Nos. 2-9 (AO 8636-8643), which are marked in the main Louvre catalogue as "de Tell Asmar?", nothing is known about the provenience of any of the texts here published. The evidence that these eight texts actually come from the Diyala River area is provided under No. 2 (AO 8636).

I can add no further information concerning the provenience of the texts No. 1 (AO 7983), 10-12 (AO 8959, 8960, 8961), and 13 (AO 10330).

The main question is the provenience of two texts, Nos. 14-15 (AO 11130, 11131), acquired by the Louvre Museum in 1927, and of one hundred and fifty-five texts, Nos. 16-170 (AO 11254-11413), acquired in 1929. The latter collection actually includes one-hundred and sixty texts, of which AO 11276 has been published previously by J. Nougayrol, "Conjuration ancienne contre Samana," AOr XVII/2 (1949) 213-226 and plates III-IV, while AO 11393, 11401, 11407, and 11408 have been excluded here because they are from the Ur III period.

A superficial glance at the major group of texts published in this volume immediately will bring to mind parallel texts published earlier in Nikolski, Dok. II Nos. 1-89, Hackman, BIN VIII passim, Donald in MCS IX, and in many scattered places. In addition, I have transliterated about two hundred texts of the same types in the Yale Babylonian Collection, Iraq Museum, and in the private possession of Dr. H. Serota of Chicago.

Scholars who have commented on these texts have taken for granted that they come from Umma. Thus Nikolski, Dok. II pp. 3f., Thureau-Dangin in RA VIII (1911) p. 154, Stephens in Hackman, BIN VIII p. 7, Sollberger in BO XVI (1959) pp. 114f., and M. Lambert in RA LIX (1965) p. 61; the last three in comments to the BIN VIII texts.

There is much confusion about the dating of this large and incongruous group of texts, and scholars often date texts from the classical Sargonic and even late Sargonic periods to the Pre-Sargonic period. Actually, three different chronological subdivisions should be distinguished within this group of texts, namely Pre-Sargonic, classical Sargonic, and late Sargonic.

To the Pre-Sargonic period belong texts dated to Lugalzagesi, ensi of Umma (and later king of Uruk), such as BIN VIII 26, 82, and 86, and all other texts related to them by prosopography, epigraphy, and other considerations. These texts certainly come from Umma. No texts in this volume belong to the Pre-Sargonic period.

To the classical Sargonic period belong texts dated to Narâm-Sin and Šar-kali-šarrī and all other texts related to them by prosopography, epigraphy, and other considerations. This period is represented by many texts in BIN VIII and this volume. The assignment of these texts to Umma has been frequently taken for granted, but never documented.

To the time after Šar-kali-šarrī, or to the so-called Gutian period, belong the mu-iti texts and parallels, many of which are found in this volume. Their Umma origin is assured.

The following texts contain materials important for the dating and provenience of the texts published in this volume and related texts from elsewhere:

a) MAD IV 14 (= AO 11130:6 and 11): mu Na-ra-am-
^{d}EN.ZU in-da-pa "he swore by the name of NS."
Line 22 has reference to the place IN^{KI}.

b) BIN VIII 162:5: mu Na-ra-am-^{d}EN.ZU-šè
"(oath) by the name of NS."

c) BIN VIII 164:2f.: mu Na-ra-am-^{d}EN.ZU lugal
A-ga-dè^{KI} in-pa "he swore by the name of NS.,
king of Akkad," and l. 24 mu lugal in-pa
"he swore by the name of the king." Line 7
lists GIŠ.MI sanga IN^{KI} "Gissu, the sanga of
IN^{KI}."

d) BIN VIII 167:14: mu lugal in-pa "he swore
by the name of the king (= NS.)." Line 7
lists GIŠ.MI sanga IN^{KI}.

e) MAD IV 15 (= AO 11131:10f.): mu Sar-ga-lí-
LUGAL-rí lugal A-ga-dè^{KI}-ka .... in-da-[pa]
"he swore by Škš., king of Akkad."

f) NBC 10197 twice: zi Sar-ga-lí-LUGAL-rí
lugal A-ga-dè^{KI} in-dí(m)-pa "he swore by the
life of Škš., king of Akkad." Text related
to a), e), and g).

g) NBC 10202: [m]u Sar-ga-lí-LUGAL-r[í] "by
the name of Škš." Text related to a), e),
and f).

h) BIN VIII 242:4f. and 11 list GIŠ.MI and
Nam-maḫ. Cf. GIŠ.MI sanga IN^{KI} under c)
and d).

i) MAD IV 158 (= AO 11398:9f.): mu lugal-šè
mu Nam-maḫ-[šè] "by the name of the king
(= Škš.?), by the name of Nammaḫ."

j) MAD IV 170 (= AO 11413:1f.): [m]u lugal-šè
[m]u sanga IN^{KI}-šè "by the name of the king
(= Škš.?), by the name of the sanga of IN^{KI}."

k) BIN VIII 157:11 has Nam-maḫ GAR-en₅-si
"Nammaḫ the ensi-designate?," while the
parallel text BIN VIII 155:14 has simply
sanga.

l) BIN VIII 155:14, see k).

m) JAOS LXXXVIII p. 58 (= 6 NT 112 and 662): two
texts from Nippur dealing with precious objects list Nam-maḫ en₅-si-ke₄ "Nammaḫ, the
ensi" and bear the date mu Sar-ga-lí-LUGAL-ri
PÙ.ŠA-Eš₄-dar GÌR.NITA é ᵈEn-líl dù-da
bí-gub-ba-a mu-ab-uš-a "the year after Škš.
appointed Puzur-Eštar, the governor-general,
to build the temple of Enlil."

n) YOS I 13: u(d)-ba Ià(NI)-ar-la-ga-an lugal
Gu-ti-um-kam .... Nam-maḫ-ni en₅-si Umma^{KI}-
ke₄ "at the time of Jarlagan, king of
Gutium ...., Nammaḫni, ensi of Umma."

o) MAD IV 68 (= AO 11307:13): u(d)-ba En-an-
na-túm en₅-si Umma^{KI} "at the time of
Enanatum, ensi of Umma."

p) Scheil, CRAI 1911 p. 319: Lugal-an-na-túm
en₅-si Umma^{KI}-ke₄ .... u(d)-ba Si-ù-um
lugal Gu-ti-um-kam "Lugalanatum, ensi of
Umma ...., at the time of Ši?um, king of
Gutium."

Central Government	Provincial Administration	IN^{KI}
a) Narâm-Sin		IN^{KI}
b) Narâm-Sin		
c) Narâm-Sin		Gissu sanga IN^{KI}
d) lugal (= Narâm-Sin)		Gissu sanga IN^{KI}
e) Šar-kali-šarrī		
f) Šar-kali-šarrī		
g) Šar-kali-šarrī		
h)	Nammaḫ	Gissu
i) lugal (= Šar-kali-šarrī?)	Nammaḫ	
j) lugal (= Šar-kali-šarrī?)		sanga IN^{KI}
k)	Nammaḫ GAR-ensi	
l)		sanga
m) Šar-kali-šarrī	Nammaḫ ensi (at Nippur)	
n) Jarlagan	Nammaḫni ensi of Umma	
o)	Enanatum ensi of Umma	
p) Ši'um	Lugalanatum ensi of Umma	

The entries listed above under a) to p) are
presented again in the chart on page xiii. The
order of the entries both in the list and the chart
is approximately chronological.

The entries in the chart are grouped under
three headings. The "Central Government" represents
the kings of Akkad and Gutium, "Provincial Administra-
tion" represents the governors of the provinces, and
"IN^{KI}" stands for the sangas of IN^{KI}.

Outside of the texts listed under a) to p), the
site IN^{KI} appears in the texts from Nippur (TMH V
49:5 and 88 ii 1) and of unknown provenience (BIN
VIII 67:11, 31 and 125:7). Cf. also Ur-dingir-ra-na?
sanga IN^{KI} on a Sargonic seal of unknown origin
(OIP XXII 96), and the personal names IN^{KI}-dùg or
IN-ki-dùg (A 25412, Pre-Sargonic, and PBS IX 50,
Sargonic) and Lú-IN^{KI} (Sumer XV p. 23 No. 3 and Pls.
I-II). The site of IN^{KI}, the reading and location
of which are unknown, ceases to exist after the
Sargonic period. The site may have been famous for
its sanctuary, as there is an obvious connection
between the sangas of IN^{KI} and the provincial
governors.

We shall start the discussion with the late
Sargonic texts containing the mu-iti dates and
follow it up with the discussion of the texts of
the classical Sargonic period.

Eighty-three texts in this volume bear a so-
called mu-iti date. The usual form is x mu, x iti,
rarely also x mu (AO 11321, 11361, 11366, etc.) and

x iti (AO 11260, 11278, etc.). In texts published elsewhere also the form x mu, x iti, x ud appears, as in the bread and beer texts of MCS IX 234, 235, 241, etc., and in other groups of texts in Dok. II.

Certain groups of texts use the mu-iti dates more frequently than the others. Thus of the eighty-three texts in this volume, fifty-nine deal with animals and skins, and twenty-one with grain, mainly threshed barley, while only three texts (AO 11363, 11373, 11403) deal with extraneous matters.

The highest number of the year recorded in the mu-iti dates known to me from published and unpublished texts, is twenty-five (AO 11272, 11283, 11345, 11365), but there are other texts from the years twenty-three, twenty-two, and twenty-one.

No text with a mu-iti date known to me has a reference to any Sargonic king or a Gutian ruler, even though Gutians are mentioned in the bread and beer texts bearing a mu-iti date, as in Frank, SKT 43 rev., MCS IX 234 rev., and Dr. Serota A 14 rev.

Against scholars who date the mu-iti texts to the Pre-Sargonic or classical Sargonic periods, for years I have argued in favor of the late Sargonic or Gutian date of those texts. In MAD II[1] p. 16 = MAD II[2] p. 11 my arguments were based on epigraphic considerations and on the references to Gutians in the mu-iti texts. However, in a supplementary note in MAD II[2] p. 208 I stated that the late Sargonic date "seems confirmed by the occurrence of a PN ^{d}Na-ra-am-^{d}EN.Z[U-í-lí?] on an unpublished tablet

bearing the date 2 MU 5 ITI 9 UD in the possession
of Dr. Serota of Chicago. The name in question can-
not be simply Narâm-Sin since the tablet deals with
administrative matters concerning private individuals.
The name is composed of a royal name, here deified,
plus an unknown predicate." My suggested recon-
struction has been splendidly confirmed by the
occurrence of a clear ^{d}Na-ra-am-^{d}EN.ZU-i-li in line
13 of a mu-iti text published recently by Donald,
MCS IX 235.

It is obvious that the existence of texts with
mu-iti dates having no reference to Sargonic or
Gutian rulers points to a time in the late Sargonic
period during which the control of the central government either was very weak or ceased altogether in
the area which gave rise to the mu-iti system of
dating. The question as to whether the number
attached to mu "year" represents the year of an era
counted from some important event or the year of the
tenure of the office of a local ruler, ensi, or even
sanga, must be left open for the present.

To the same date as the mu-iti texts must be
assigned all the texts not having a mu-iti date, but
related to the mu-iti texts by prosopography, epigraphy, and other considerations.

Thus the mu-iti texts which mention Ama-é (wife
of Ur-^{d}Šara), such as AO 11367 and 11373, are clearly
related to several undated texts referring to the
activities of that woman, such as AO 11255, 11259,
11280, 11304, 11307, 11312, and 11388. The text AO

11312 in turn mentions Ur-^{d}Nin-^{d}NAGAR.GÍD sipa, who
is obviously the same as Ur-^{d}Nin-^{d}NAGAR.GÍD udul of
the mu-iti texts AO 11277 and 11281. Similar connections can be established among the texts employing
the measure gur-sag-gál-dúl/kug; see under Writing.
All these connections, based on the occurrence of
identical personal names, paternity, professions,
and measures, are strengthened by considerations of
identical types of texts (deposition of commodities,
accounts of cattle, of sheepskins, etc.) with and
without the mu-iti date.

Especially important for the late Sargonic date
of the mu-iti and related texts is AO 11307, a deposition text with reference to Ama-é, which contains
in place of the mu-iti date, a date reading u(d)-ba
En-an-na-DU en$_5$-si Umma^{KI} "at the time of Enanatum,
ensi of Umma." This type of dating is characteristic
of the late Sargonic period.

The Umma provenience of the mu-iti and related
texts is based on several considerations. Umma and
Zabala(m) are two of the most commonly occurring
geographic names in these texts. Zabala(m) (written
regularly AB.INNIN^{KI}) is localized at modern Ibzaiḫ,
about six miles north of Umma; for the reading
Zabala(m) cf. the spelling AB.INNIN^{KI}-la in Dok. II
49 rev., a mu-iti text. Several epigraphic features
of the Umma texts are taken up below under Writing,
the most important of these being the form of the
fractions for 1/2 and 1/4.

While little doubt remains about the Umma pro-

venience of the late Sargonic texts with the mu-iti
date and of all the related texts, the question of
the provenience of the classical Sargonic texts in
this volume and of the related texts elsewhere remains in doubt.

The first question to be posed is whether the
one hundred and fifty-seven texts published in this
volume, two of which (AO 11130 and 11131) represent
the Acquisition David, Dec. 22, 1927 and the rest
(AO 11254-11413) the Acquisition Genouillac, June 22,
1929 in the Louvre catalogues, come from the same
site or not. If they do, then there is no problem.
Since the late Sargonic texts in this collection come
from Umma, the texts of the classical Sargonic period
should also be assigned to Umma.

For many years I have taken for granted the Umma
derivation of all the one hundred and fifty-seven
texts of the Louvre Collection. Now I am not so sure.
First of all, it should be noted that the text AO
11254 of the Acquisition Genouillac, June 22, 1929, is
written in Akkadian, not in Sumerian as all other
texts of that collection in this volume are. Con-
sequently, we must assume that at least the text AO
11254 does not come from Umma. Further, there are
unmistakable parallels between some texts in our
collection and a group of texts in BIN VIII which
Stephens in BIN VIII p. 7 and Sollberger in BO p. 115a
assigned to Nippur. In my judgment, the evidence
linking this group of BIN VIII texts with Nippur needs
detailed corroboration.

The political-historical information which can
be gathered from our texts and parallels is presented
in the chart on p. xiii. The information concerning
Nammaḫ, ensi of Nippur, of AS 17 No. 5, discussed
op. cit. pp. 5f. and copied on p. 21, is not listed
in that chart, since epigraphically this text comes
from the Pre-Sargonic or early Sargonic period. There
are several problems in the chart. Is Nammaḫ, who is
listed four times, one and the same person? Was he
governor at Nippur and also at Umma? Is Nammaḫ the
same person as Nammaḫni, ensi of Umma at the time of
the Gutian king Jarlagan? What is the location of
IN^{KI} in relation to Nippur or Umma?

These problems affect the provenience of a rela-
tively small number of texts in our collection of
one hundred and fifty-seven texts. Since the eighty-
three mu-iti texts and about forty related texts come
from Umma, the uncertainty about the provenience
affects only about thirty texts, including the
important group of nineteen witnessed contracts.

Tablets

With the exception of AO 11413, which is a
perforated clay cone, all texts are written on clay
tablets. All texts are written in single columns
with the exception of four two-column texts, namely
AO 11254, 11315, 11391, and 11392. I have had some
difficulties in establishing the color of the tablets,
especially those described as buff, light buff, or
gray.

Writing

Several epigraphic peculiarities of the texts published in this volume can be noted.

Contrary to the general rule of cuneiform writing with respect to word division, words which are normally written in one line are often separated, as in the following cases: [18]PN sipa- [19]da i̇-da-sig$_7$ (AO 11267, and similarly in 11297:9f., 11315 rev. i 2f., and 11339:7f.); bar [6]zú-si- [7]ka-ta (AO 11372); and [3]a-šà Àm-ma- [4]ta mu-$_{DU}^{DU}$ (AO 11376).

Certain forms of signs are standardized in our texts, such as ⬦ for iti (AO 11350, 11378, 11383, etc.), ⟨ for šuš (AO 11262, etc.), and 🀫 for u$_8$ (AO 11257, etc.). The form $_{DU}^{DU}$ occurs in mu-$_{DU}^{DU}$ (AO 11271:3, 11376:4) and in Da-pi-$_{DU}^{DU}$ (AO 11391:9), against the standard mu-DU.DU (AO 11396:15, etc.); cf. also the writing of lú over dingir in ud $_{dingir}^{lú}$ -ma dù-da-a in AO 11392 ii 4, which is un-understandable to me. The form ⊱ for pi, occurring three times in AO 11131, is found also in BIN VIII 174:5, 293 i 1', iii 21, and NBC 10202. The form SAL.SI.ÁŠ.GÀR occurs six times in AO 11261:6, 11262:8, 11279:5, 12, and 11315 i 5, ii 2, as against the standard SAL.ÁŠ.GÀR in other texts here and elsewhere. The form U.EDIN for baḫar$_x$ "potter" is found twice in our texts in AO 11274:14 and 11387:9, as it is frequently elsewhere, against the simple EDIN in AO 11343:7. The sign ⬠ following gemé in AO 11271:9

is new to me completely. For parallels to the writing
túg ti in AO 11303:3 in place of the expected túg bal
in AO 11308:3 and elsewhere, see MAD V pp. xxiiif.
The question of the sign form GUD plus a vertical
(or oblique) wedge in É-gud of AO 11257:13 will be
taken up, with many other parallels, in the third
edition of MAD II. The sign EŠ in the geographic
name Na-EŠ-dù-a (see Index, also in ITT III/2 p. 50,
5852 and Ist. Mus. Lagash 30221) may have the syl-
labic value aš$_x$, as shown by Na-áš-dù-a^{KI} (ITT II/1
3704).

   "Wrong" order of signs is attested in the
following cases: Ezen-DUMU.ZI.AN.KA (AO 11321:6)
for Ezen-^{d}Dumu-zi-ka; 1 lá igi-4-KUG.GÁL.GÍN (AO
11363:1) for 1 lá igi-4-gál kug gín; 186.2.0 GÁL.ŠE.
GUR.SAG (AO 11375:1) for 186.2.0 še gur-sag-gál; and
UD.ḪU.MI.AN.IM (AO 11392 rev. i 3) for ^{d}Utu-IM.MI^{mušen}.
In a text from Tell Asmar? we find the sequence
DU+UD.A (AO 8641:6) for UD.DU.A = É.A.

   The dry measure of capacity gur-sag-gál-dúl is
known to me only from the Umma texts, such as AO
11260, 11278, 11282, 11287, 11296, 11305, 11311?,
11329, 11343, 11360, 11381, 11384, Iraq Mus. 13381,
and MCS IX 236 and 238; the measure gur-sag-gál-kug
(AO 11273) is unattested elsewhere. Almost all these
texts have a mu-iti date.

   In the first line of the text lá-ni with the
following numbers takes an unusual form in the sheep
texts, with the signs lá-ni forming an umbrella over
the round numbers. See AO 11272, 11291, 11297, and
11385.

The texts generally use round, not pointed, forms of numbers. But it is interesting to note that several mu-iti texts of the late Sargonic period use exclusively pointed numbers, just as the texts of the following Ur III period. Cf. AO 11301, 11318, 11321, 11324, 11330, 11331, 11348, 11372, 11377, 11380, 11386, and 11387. The vertical pointed numbers are often slightly slanted to the left. Pointed numbers are used regularly in the mu-iti dates, and in years denoting the age of animals, (as in AO 11266:2, 4, 11277:2, 3, 4, 8, 11281:2-6, and 11299:1, 4). Occasionally texts which use generally round numbers also have pointed numbers. Cf. with lá-ni in AO 11265:5, 11272:14 and 15, 11314:9, 11385:8; with zag-nu-šuš in AO 11396:4; with šu-nigín in AO 11255: 18; with ma-na in AO 11255:18 (in contrast to a rounded form of 1 gú); with gín in AO 11392:9; with túg in AO 11406:1-4; with sum in AO 11370:1, 2; with guruš in AO 11410 passim; with gán in AO 11394 passim; and with kuš in AO 11332:8 (in contrast to a rounded form in line 1).

A number of texts in this collection have two signs in the form of ⊁ and ⋇ , which I should like to interpret (provisionally) as fractions for 1/2 and 1/4, respectively. Both forms occur as subdivisions of the dry measure gur in AO 11264, 11270, 11311, 11313, and 11381 (a mu-iti text). The first form only occurs as a subdivision of the measure of length gar-du in AO 11405 and 11409, with the latter text using the form also for a fraction of the measure of

area iku. Cf. also the forms in the difficult text
AO 11369, which may be a school exercise.

Outside of our collection, these two forms of
fractions occur apparently only in texts from Umma.
The second form occurs as a subdivision of gur in
Bab. VIII Pl. VIII, Pupil 32, and in several unpublished texts in the Ashmolean Museum, all of
Ur III date. The first form is found frequently as
a subdivision of the measure of area iku in BIN VIII
82, 86, and 90 of the time of Lugalzagesi, of the
liquid measure silà in the Sargonic text BIN VIII 329,
and of the measure of weight ma-na in an unpublished
Sargonic text Iraq Mus. 5592/8.

Language

The first thirteen texts in this volume, which
originated either in the Diyala River area or are of
unknown origin, are all written either in Akkadian or
in noncommittal logograms (AO 8642 and 10330) which
can be read in Akkadian. All the other texts in this
volume are written in Sumerian. The text AO 11254,
which represents the first text in the Acquisition
Genouillac, June 22, 1929 collection, is written in
Akkadian, and its contents and prosopography show no
relation to the other texts in the collection. This
text therefore must have originated in an area other
than the Sumerian texts in the collection.

Contents

Many texts in this volume can be grouped by
contents. The largest group of texts deals with

animals, which are mainly sheep and goats, but also
bovines. Many texts deal with grain, especially
threshed barley. Nineteen witnessed contracts make
up a very important group of legal texts.

Omitting from consideration insignificant
variants, such as udu-u$_8$-ama for u$_8$-ama, these are
the terms used for sheep and goats in our texts:

	Sheep	Goats
Grown female:	u$_8$-ama	úz-ama
Grown male:	udu-nita	máš-gal
Young female:	SAL-sila$_4$ ša-dùg	SAL.ÁŠ.GÀR ša-dùg
Young male:	sila$_4$-nita ša-dùg	máš-nita ša-dùg

The following is a list of the witnessed contracts in this volume: AO 8638, 11130, 11131,
11265, 11274, 11290, 11307, 11309, 11316, 11317,
11319, 11320, 11389, 11390, 11391, 11392, 11395,
11398, and 11412. All these texts may or may not
represent one single archive coming from one site,
with the exception of AO 8638, which originated in
the Diyala River area. These nineteen texts deal
with the purchase of individuals, fields, and
different commodities. In addition, we find two
other witnessed texts, AO 11363 and 11413, which do
not deal with acquisitions. The contracts published
in this volume show certain relationships with the
contracts published in BIN VIII and treated by M.
Lambert in RA LIX (1965) pp. 61-72 and 115-126.

TEXTS IN TRANSLITERATION

1. (AO 7983)

Acquisition Ihler, between 1921 and 1922. Dark gray.
26 × 24 × 10 mm. Receipt of barley. Plate I.

        1) 5(GUR) 2(PI) 40+2 SILÀ
           ŠE GUR.SAG.GÁL
        2) È
        3) Ì-lí-sa-lik
    Rev. 4) Me-me (f.n.)
        5) dam-ḫur

2. (AO 8636)

Acquisition Géjou, 1923, from Tell Asmar? Brown-
gray. 60 × 44 × 17 mm. Account of silver, an
equid, oxen, and barley. Plate I.

According to the Louvre catalogue, eight texts,
AO 8636-8643, are said to come possibly from Tell
Asmar. This can be supported by the following
evidence: si-ib-šum (AO 8637 and 8643), compared
with šibšum, found only in the texts of the Diyala
Region; gu-su$_4$-ra-im (AO 8638), compared with
kušurrā'um, found only in the Diyala texts; Tu-tu[KI]
(AO 8640), a geographic name in the Diyala Region;
and A-bí-[d]Tišpak (AO 8637), known in the Diyala
Region.

        1) 2/3 KUG.BABBAR ŠA.PI
        2) 1 ANŠE.BAR.AN NITA
        3) 4 GUD
        4) LÁ.NI
        5) 180 (more probable than 3) ŠE GUR

6) [i]n? GUR A-ga-dè^{KI}

7) ⌈É⌉? Ḫa-lum (or ⌈X⌉-ḫa-LUM)

Rev.   (uninscribed)

3. (AO 8637)

Acquisition Géjou, 1923, from Tell Asmar? Brown.
49 × 41 × 17 mm. Account of barley. Plate I.

1) 4(GUR) 2(PI) ŠE GUR

2) A-bí-^{d}Tišpak

3) 16(GUR) É-gal

4) 3(GUR) 3(PI) I-da-da

5) 3(GUR) 3(PI) Pù-DINGIR

   (double line)

6) si-ib-šum

7) šu A-za-GÀR

Rev.   (uninscribed)

4. (AO 8638)

Acquisition Géjou, 1923, from Tell Asmar? Dark gray.
46 × 31 × 15 mm. Witnessed contract concerning the
purchase of gold. Plate I.

1) 15 KUG.BABBAR GÍN

2) a-na NÍG.ŠÁM

3) 2 KUG.GI GÍN

4) I-gu-núm

5) DAM.GÀR

6) iš-dè Nu-ni-tum

7) im-ḫur

8) 1 En-na-na

       9) DUMU DINGIR-⌈a⌉-zu

Rev. 10) 1 DINGIR-ba-ni

      11) šu A-ba

      12) 1 É-a-ba-lik

      13) NAR

      14) 1 Wa-dar-ì-li

      15) NAR

      16) AB+ÁŠ.AB+ÁŠ

      17) gu-su₄-ra-im

5. (AO 8639)

Acquisition Géjou, 1923, from Tell Asmar? Dark gray.
34 × 32 × 14 mm. Receipt of sheep, goats, and silver.
Plate II.

       1) 40 LÁ 1 UDU.NITA

       2) 3 MÁŠ

       3) 11 KUG.BABBAR GÍN

       4) ENGAR

Rev. 5) Pù-sa-GI (more probable than
              Pù-gi-sa)
           (space)

       6) MU.DU

6. (AO 8640)

Acquisition Géjou, 1923, from Tell Asmar? Brown.
36 × 30 × 14 mm. Account of barley. Plate II.

       1) 2(GUR) 2(PI) ŠE GUR

       2) Be-lí-GÀR

       3) 1(GUR) 1(PI) ŠE GUR

4) Be-lí-lí

5) ŠE šu Tu-tu^{KI}

Rev. (uninscribed)

7. (AO 8641)

Acquisition Géjou, 1923, from Tell Asmar? Brown.
36 × 30 × 14 mm. Issue of barley. Plate II.

1) 3(GUR) 3(PI) ŠE GUR

2) Pù-DINGIR

3) 1(GUR) 2(PI) ŠE GUR

4) É-a-ra-bí

Rev. (space)

5) (erasure)

6) È(wr. DU+UD).A

8. (AO 8642)

Acquisition Géjou, 1923, from Tell Asmar? Light
brown, 32 × 30 × 16 mm. Account of goatskins.
Plate II.

1) 10 KUŠ MÁŠ

2) Ar-na-ba

3) 5 NI-za-za

4) 5 Si-ku-sum

Rev. 5) 2 A-bí-SU

(rest uninscribed)

9. (AO 8643)

Acquisition Géjou, 1923, from Tell Asmar? Dark
gray. 22 × 22 × 11 mm. Receipt of barley. Plate
III.

-6-

1) 5 ŠE GUR

2) Ú-ba-ru

3) AB+ÁŠ.URU^{KI}

Rev. 4) si-ib-šum

(space)

5) MU.DU

10. (AO 8959)

Acquisition 1924. Reddish-brown. 68 × 41 × 18 mm.
Account of barley. Plate IV.

1) 3(GUR) 1(PI) 20(SILÀ) ŠE

GUR.SAG.GÁL

2) in a-lí-im

3) Ì-lí-iš-da-gal

4) ú-šu-ri-dam

5) ib-ba-al-gi-it-ma

6) a-na 2(GUR) 40(SILÀ) ŠE GUR

7) in zu-ti ANŠE

8) È.PI

9) 1(PI) 20(SILÀ) ŠE SIG$_5$

Rev. 10) a-na ZÍD.GU

11) Dan-ì-li

12) im-[ḫur]

13) 10 ŠE GUR.SAG.GÁL

14) [I]-nin-la-ba

15) [DU]MU SIG$_5$-DINGIR

16) im-ḫur

17) 1(PI) Im$_x$(DU)-da-lik

18) MAŠ.NI

-7-

(space)

19) ITI Ḫa-ni-it

11. (AO 8960)

Acquisition 1924. Brown. 92 × 40 × 30 mm. Account of barley. Plate IV.

   1) 180+30 ŠE GUR.SAG.GÁL

   2) I-da-[DING]IR

   3) 180 ŠE GUR.SAG.GÁL

   4) Mi-su$_4$-a

   5) DUMU ⌈Ur⌉-mes

   6) 180+⌈30⌉ ŠE GUR.SAG.GÁL

   7) I-da-[DINGIR]

   8) 120 ŠE GUR.SAG.GÁL

   9) 30 ŠE GUR.SAG.GÁL (sic)

   10) šu A-ḫu-mu-bí

   11) SAG.DU$_5$

   12) I-da-DINGIR

Rev. 13) in da(𒁴𒉌)-NI

   14) GIŠ.SAG.ḪAR

   15) ù-bi-lam

   16) 60+40 ŠE GUR.SAG.GÁL

   17) NA.GADA.NA.GADA

   18) ù-bi-lu-nim

   19) 20 ŠE GUR.SAG.GÁL

   20) šu DINGIR-su-a-ḫa

   21) DUMU ⌈Na⌉-ni

   22) ⌈iš⌉-dè

   23) A-ru-um

-8-

24) ù ^{d}KA-Me-ir

25) I-da-DINGIR

26) ù Mi-su$_4$-a

27) im-ḫur-ra

12. (AO 8961)

Acquisition 1924. Dark gray. 28 × 26 × 12 mm.
Receipt of an unknown commodity.

1) 3 G[Ú x] MA.N[A ....]

2) Dam-da-[li]k (f.n.)

3) dam-ḫur

Rev. 4) [Ì]-lí-iš-da-gal

5) i-ti-in

13. (AO 10330)

Acquisition Géjou, Dec. 1925. Brown. 75 × 52 × 24
mm. Account of a beer ingredient called BAPPIR
and of flour.

1) 3(PI) BAPPIR SIG$_5$

2) 3(PI) NÍG.ḪAR.RA SIG$_5$

3) ḪAL-ì-[lum]

4) 30(SILÀ) [....]

(rest covered with salts,
unreadable)

14. (AO 11130)

Acquisition David, Dec. 22, 1927. Gray. 63 × 35 ×
17 mm. Witnessed contract concerning a field. Note
oath by Narâm-Sin. Plate V.

1) 1(iku) gán [....] UŠ

2) UŠ-[da-d]a

3) [....]

4) kúr [....]

5) Inim-ma?(𒅗)

6) [mu Na-ra-am]-^dEN.ZU

7) in-da-[p]a

8) Sá-lim-mu dumu [É]-maḫ-da-ke₄

9) bar Nin-ra-ka

10) UŠ-[da]-da

Rev. 11) mu Na-r[a-a]m-^dEN.ZU

12) in-da-pa kúr KA Nin-ra

13) Inim-ma nu-na-gá-gá-šè

(double line)

14) igi 1 Ur-du-du

15) dumu Ur-PA

16) igi 1 É-zi

17) lú Ur-zu

18) igi 1 Zag-mu A-ba-^dEn-líl

19) igi 1 Ur-PA DINGIR-ba-ni

(double line)

20) lú-ki-inim-ma-bi-me

(double line)

21) Ur-kalag-ga

22) lú-erín KU.KU(=durun-durun) IN^{KI}

L.E. 23) mu gi₄-dè pa

15. (AO 11131)

Acquisition David, Dec. 22, 1927. Dark gray.

74 × 42 × 18 mm. Witnessed contract concerning the
purchase of ten gur of dates. Note oath by Šar-kali-
šarrī. Note the form of the sign ⬦⊢ in lines 14,
18, and 25, identical with PI in níg-šam-ma-pi in
<u>BIN</u> VIII 174:5. Plate III.

1) 10 zú-lum gur kug-ta

2) ud zú-lum 1 kug gín-a?(𐎏)

3) 3(PI) 20(SILÀ) al-ág-gá

4) UŠ dumu Sag-du$_5$-ke$_4$

5) UŠ dumu SILÀ.ŠU.DU$_8$-maḫ-ra

6) kug 10 kug gín-šè

7) ì-na-sum

8) kug gán-ka še gán-bi

9) 30 še gur kug-ta gú ba-gar

10) mu Sar-ga-lí-LUGAL-rí

11) lugal A-ga-dè^{KI}-ka

12) UŠ dumu SILÀ.ŠU.DU$_8$-maḫ

13) ME-an-ni

Rev. 14) dumu Lugal-kalag-zi-pi

15) UŠ dumu Sag-du$_5$-ka-šè

16) in-da-⌈pa⌉

17) ud gán-ka še-zu 1 kug gín

18) 3 še gur-⌈ta⌉ 30 še PI gur

19) g⌈a-r⌉a-[....]

20) in-na-⌈ag⌉

21) KA-bi [al-til]

    (double line)

22) igi 1 Nin-dug$_4$-ga

23) igi 1 Lú-[x-x](⊟⊢)

         24) igi 1 ^dEn-líl-[lá]? nu-[S]AR?(▨🏳)

L.E. 25) ME-šeš-šeš dub-sar-pi

                16. (AO 11254)

Acquisition Genouillac, June 22, 1929. Two-column
tablet. Dark gray. 86 × 74 × 21 mm. Issue of
barley. Plate VI.

   i 1)   33 UDU.ḪI.A 4(PI) 20(SILÀ)
     2)   ŠÁM-su-nu ŠE(sic) 28(GUR)
          3(PI) GUR
     3)   a-na A-ga-de_•^{KI}
     4)   30 UDU.ḪI.A 3(PI) 20(SILÀ)
     5)   ŠÁM-su-nu 20 ŠE GUR
     6)   5 UDU.ḪI.A 2(PI)
     7)   ŠÁM-su-nu 2 ŠE GUR
     8)   a-na BÀD LUGAL
  ii 1)   3 ŠE GUR
     2)   Lú-^dAš(𒌋)-šir-gi₄
     3)   1 ŠE GUR
     4)   SAG.DU₅
     5)   3(GUR) 1(PI) 30(SILÀ) ŠE GUR
          a-na KÙ SAG.DU₅
     6)   3(GUR) 2(PI) 30(SILÀ) ŠE GUR
          a-na KÙ É LUGAL
     7)   35 UDU
     8)   a-na KÙ-šu-nu
Rev. i 1)   5 ŠE GUR
     2)   [š]u 2 ITI
     3)   3(PI) Im-ta
     4)   3(PI) Ur-zu

5) 3(PI) Zu-zu

6) 1(PI) I-ti-^dDa-gan

7) 1(PI) E-lam

ii 1) [ŠU.NIGÍ]N 68(GUR) 3(PI) ŠE GUR

2) È.A

17. (AO 11255)

Acquisition Genouillac, June 22, 1929. Light buff.
57 × 35 × 16 mm. Account of wool. Plate V.

1) 20 síg ma-na

2) Ama-é-e

3) Barag-nita-ra

4) ša₆-ma ì-na-dug₄

5) 15 síg ma-na

6) Ama-é-e

7) Barag-nita-ra

8) ì-na-sum

9) 20 lá 2 síg ma-na

Rev. 10) Ama-é-e

11) Barag-nita-ra

12) AB.INNIN^{KI}-šè

13) gin-ni ì-na-sum

14) 8 síg ma-na

15) Ama-é-e

16) Barag-nita-da u(d)-bi-ta

17) ì-da-tuku-àm

(double line)

U.E. 18) šu-nigín 1(▷) síg gú 1(◁) ma-na

-13-

18. (AO 11256)

Acquisition Genouillac, June 22, 1929. Light buff.
70 × 44 × 19 mm. Almost completely effaced. Text
treats of animals. End: ì-da-sig₇, (space), 6 mu
3 iti.

19. (AO 11257)

Acquisition Genouillac, June 22, 1929. Light buff-
gray. 58 × 45 × 19 mm. Account of sheep and goats.
Plate VII.

	1)	32 u₈-ama
	2)	40 lá 1 udu-nita
	3)	11 SAL-sila₄ šà-dùg
	4)	10 lá 1 sila₄-nita šà-dùg
	5)	14 ùz KU
	6)	5 máš-gal-gal
	7)	8 SAL.ÁŠ.<GÀR> šà-dùg
Lo.E.	8)	2 máš-nita šà-dùg
Rev.		(space)
	9)	šu-nigín 91 udu
	10)	šu-nigín 30 lá 1 ùz
	11)	udu Ur-^{d}Šara-ka-kam
	12)	En-an-ni e-da-sig₇
	13)	udu ur₄-ra É-gud(wr. GUD+𒑱) ra-àm
	14)	10 mu 8 iti

20. (AO 11258)

Acquisition Genouillac, June 22, 1929. Light buff-
gray. 56 × 33 × 16. Account of goats.

1) ⌈50⌉ lá 3 ùz-ama

2) 10 SAL.ÁŠ.GÀR šà-dùg

3) 10 máš šà-dùg

4) 15 máš-gal-gal

   (double line)

5) šu-nigín 82 ùz gub-ba

6) Ur-^{d}Šara-ka-kam

7) ^{d}Utu-mu sipa-da

8) ì-da-sig$_7$

Rev. 9) Barag-sì-ga a-gar-ra-bi ba-ag

   (space)

10) 11 mu 7 iti

21. (AO 11259)

Acquisition Genouillac, June 22, 1929. Light buff.
69 × 45 × 19 mm. Issue of barley.

1) 60 lá? 13? še [gur]-sag-gál

2) Ur-^{d}En-dím-gi[g]?

3) 15(gur) Ur-ša$_6$-g[a] SILÀ.ŠU.DU$_8$

4) 10(gur) Ur-^{d}Nagar UŠ.KU

5) 46(gur) 2(pi) Me-zu dub-sar

6) 6(gur) Ur-gu Ur-du-du (sic)

7) 16(gur) Ú-da

8) 10(gur) Ama-é-e

9) šu-ba-ti

Rev. 10) 5(gur) Íd-ḫi-nun nu-gig

11) 20(gur) Ur-šubur GIŠ.TÚG.KAR.DU

   (space)

12) šu-nigín 120+40+[10]?+⌈5⌉(gur)

   2(pi) še gur-sag-gál

13) še zi-ga

14) Ur-zu? dí[m]? (wr. Ur- 𒌨 𒂖)

(space)

15) 5? mu 4 iti

22. (AO 11260)

Acquisition Genouillac, June 22, 1929. Light buff.
65 × 36 × 18 mm. Account of threshed barley.

1) 10(gur) 3(pi) še gur-sag-gál-dùl

2) Ur-^{d}En-líl-lá

3) 480(or 540)+40(gur) lá 20(silà)

še gur

4) Ur-dam

5) 190 lá 1 še gur

6) Lugal-an-ni

7) 16 še gur

8) Inim-zi-da

9) še-giš-ra-a

Rev. 10) sig$_7$ BAR.DU

11) UŠ.KU šu-i(𒋗)

12) šu-ba-ti

(space)

13) 4 iti

23. (AO 11261)

Acquisition Genouillac, June 22, 1929. Light brown.
69 × 45 × 18 mm. Account of sheep and goats.

1) 31+[x u$_8$-ama]

2) 13+[x udu]-nita
3) [x sila₄-ni]ta ša-dùg
4) 10+[x SAL-si]la₄ ša-dùg
5) 23+[x] ùz-ama
6) 3 SAL.SI.ÁŠ.GÀR ša-dùg
7) 30+1? máš
   (double line)
8) šu-nigín 125 ùz-udu
9) Ur-ᵈŠara-ka-kam
10) 6 u₈-ama
Rev. 11) 2 udu-nita
12) 10 ùz-ama
13) 7 máš
   (double line)
14) šu-nigín 25 ùz-udu
15) Ur-ᵈEN.ZU-ka-kam
16) udu ME.NI
17) ᵈUtu-mu sipa
   (space)
18) 6 mu 3 iti

24. (AO 11262)

Acquisition Genouillac, June 22, 1929. Light buff.
63 × 41 × 17 mm. Account of goatskins, goats, and
sheep. Plate VII.

1) 2 kuš ùz zag-šuš
2) 1 kuš máš zag-šuš
3) 1 máš zag-nu-šuš
4) 1 sila₄-nita zag-nu-šuš

-17-

5) Ur-^{d}Šara-ka-kam

6) 1 udu-nita zag-šuš

7) Lugal-KA-kam

8) 1 SAL.SI.ÀŠ.GÀR zag-nu-šuš

9) Si-dù sipa

10) 1 kuš ùz zag-šuš

Rev. 11) Ur-^{d}EN.ZU-kam

12) 1 máš Ur-^{d}Šara dub-sar dingir-ra

13) ^{d}Utu-mu sipa

14) Na-EŠ(𒐗)-dù-a

(space)

15) 5 mu 4 iti

25. (AO 11263)

Acquisition Genouillac, June 22, 1929. Light gray.
56 × 35 × 18 mm. Pointed forms of numbers. Units
for 1-9 gur are written vertically. Account of barley?
of 9 different persons in 3 groups.

1) 34(gur) ⌈ME-^{d}IM⌉

2) 16(gur) Mušen-dù

3) 15(gur) Lugal-ab(𒍝𒊑)

4) 10(gur) KA-šè

5) 20 lá 2(gur) Da-da

6) Ur-^{d}TUR

7) 30 lá 2(gur) Lugal-si

8) 25(gur) Ur-^{GIŠ}gigir

9) 10(gur) Ur-^{d}TUR

10) Lugal-KA

Rev. 11) 10(gur) Ur-mes

12) Ur-du$_{6}$

-18-

26. (AO 11264)

Acquisition Genouillac, June 22, 1929. Light gray.
56 × 38 × 16 mm. Pointed forms of numbers. 60 gur
is written horizontally; units for 1-9 gur are written
vertically (slightly slanted). Account of barley.

        1) 50+[x še] gur-sag-[gál]

        2) UŠ.KU Ama-UM+ME.GA

        3) 65(gur) 𐏑 še gur

        4) Lugal-níg

        5) 55 še gur

        6) Á-kal-li

        7) 66 še gur

        8) É-e

   Rev.   (uninscribed)

27. (AO 11265)

Acquisition Genouillac, June 22, 1929. Light buff.
57 × 34 × 20 mm. Reverse badly effaced. Witnessed
contract concerning sheep, goats, and wool. Plate
VIII.

        1) 16 u_8

        2) 21 udu-nita

        3) 8 ùz

        4) 4 máš-nita

        5) 50 lá 1 síg ma-na (pointed forms
           of numbers)

        6) lá-ni-àm

        7) En-an-ni

        8) [....]

  Rev. 9) SU .[...]

10) a-šà dé-a Ur-e? DU-ma

11) ⌜udu A⌝.LÁ.A 20 lá 1 (pointed numbers)

12) í[b-t]a-zi

13) Da-da? šeš-mu

14) ⌜....⌝

15) ⌜....⌝

16) lú-ki-inim-[ma-me]

L.E. 17) níg-ŠID-bi ì-til 15 mu 10 iti

28. (AO 11266)

Acquisition Genouillac, June 22, 1929. Light buff. 62 × 39 × 18 mm. Pointed forms of numbers in front of (mu). Account of cattle, sheep, and goats.

1) 3 gud-giš

2) 1 gud 3 (mu)

3) 3 áb

4) 1 áb 1 (mu)

5) 3 amar da-ba

6) 5 u_8-ama

7) 1 SAL-sila$_4$ šà-dùg

8) 33 ùz-ama

9) 3 SAL.ÁŠ.GÀR šà-dùg

10) 1 máš šà-dùg

Rev. (space)

11) šu-nigin 43 udu-ùz gub-ba

12) Ur-^{d}EN.ZU-kam

29. (AO 11267)

Acquisition Genouillac, June 22, 1929. Light buff.
80 × 48 × 21 mm. Account of sheep and goats.

1) 11 u$_8$-[ama]
2) 3 SAL-sila$_4$ ša-dùg
3) 3 sila$_4$-nita ša-dùg
4) 34 ùz-ama
5) 15 SAL.ÀŠ.GÀR ša-dùg
6) 3 máš ša-dùg
   (double line)
7) šu-nigín 70 lá 1 ùz-udu
8) Ur-^{d}Šara-ka-kam
9) 26 ùz-ama
10) 13 SAL.ÀŠ.GÀR ša-dùg
11) 2 máš ša-dùg

Rev. 12) 7 u$_8$-ama
13) 2 SAL-sila$_4$ ša-dùg
14) 1 sila$_4$-nita ša-dùg
   (double line)
15) šu-nigín 51 ùz-udu
16) udu gub-ba É.A-si$_4$-na
17) Ur-^{d}EN.ZU-ka-kam
18) A-bí-nar sipa-
19) da ì-da-sig$_7$
20) Ur-sipa-da sipa
21) na-ga-da (cf. AO 11315)
22) 2 mu 8 iti

30. (AO 11268)

Acquisition Genouillac, June 22, 1929. Light buff-

gray. 71 × 41 × 18 mm. Reverse effaced. Card catalogue reads: "An 2, 8e mois." Account of goats and
sheep.

1) 60 ùz-ama
2) 30 lá 2 SAL.ÁŠ.GÀR šà-dùg
3) 5 máš-nita šà-dùg
4) 20 lá 1 u$_8$-ama
5) 3 SAL-sila$_4$ šà-dùg
6) 4 sila$_4$-nita
   (double line)
7) šu-nigín 120 (should be 119)
   ùz-udu
8) im-si-sá-àm
9) A-bí-nar-da
10) ì-da-sig$_7$
11) Ur-sipa sipa

Rev.   (destroyed completely but for a
        trace of the iti sign at the end)

31. (AO 11269)

Acquisition Genouillac, June 22, 1929. Light buff.
68 × 42 × 19 mm. Reverse effaced. Card catalogue
reads: "An 17." Text similar to AO 11271. Account
of gifts of sheep and goats. Plate IX.

1) [x udu-nita] é .[...]
2) 2? udu-nita uru-si[g$_4$-?]
3) [x] udu-nita da GIŠ.ḪAR?
4) En-an-ni ba-DU.[DU]
5) [x] udu-nita é du$_6$-k[a]

-22-

6) Nam-ti-la-ra e-na-s[um]

7) 1 udu-nita GIŠ.AŠ(◁) ^dNisaba

   é nam-zu ÉŠ.KA

8) Nam-ti-la-ra e-na-sum

9) 2 udu-nita 1 máš gán-maḫ?(⌇⌇)

10) Gemé-è-a ba-DU.DU

11) 1 SAL-sila₄ 1 sil[a₄-nita]

Rev.   (destroyed)

32. (AO 11270)

Acquisition Genouillac, June 22, 1929. Brown-gray.
62 × 42 × 20 mm. Pointed forms of numbers. 60 gur
is written horizontally; units for 1-9 gur are
written vertically (slightly slanted). Account of
barley. Plate IX.

1) 56(gur) 大 še gur-sag-gál

2) Ur-kud

3) 70(gur) 大 še gur

4) Ama-barag

5) 77 še gur

6) Lul-gu-ag

7) 53 še gur

8) Lugal-AŠ(⌇)-ni

9) 63 še gur

10) [X-š]eš

    (rest destroyed)

Rev.   (beginning destroyed)

1') ⌈....⌉

2') 61 še gur

3') Lugal-⌈....⌉

-23-

33. (AO 11271)

Acquisition Genouillac, June 22, 1929. Light buff.
63 × 42 × 18 mm. Text similar to AO 11269. Account
of gifts of sheep and goats. Plate VIII.

    1) 3 udu-nita

    2) a-ùr-ra in-tuš?(冃)-a

    3) pisan-udu-ta mu-$_{DU}^{DU}$

    4) Nam-ti-la-ni e-zu(sic)

    5) 1 máš

    6) uru-a e nar-ka-àm

    7) dingir-ra-na-šè e-gub

    8) 1 udu-nita En-an-ni

    9) gemé ⬦ dub kaskal-ra e-na-sum

Rev. 10) 1 u$_8$ Gemé-è-a

   11) Da-da-ra

   12) e-na-sum

   13) 1 udu-nita Gemé-è-a

   14) Nam-ti-la-na-ra

   15) e-na-sum

34. (AO 11272)

Acquisition Genouillac, June 22, 1929. Light buff.
65 × 42 × 18 mm. Account of sheep and goats.

    1) lá-ni 16 u$_8$-ama

    2) 11 [udu]-nita

    3) 20 [LÁ 1 SAL]-sila$_4$

    4) 8 úz-⌈ama⌉

    5) 5 [máš-gal-gal]

    6) 3 SAL.ÁŠ.GÀR [šà-dùg]

    7) 8 máš šà-dùg

8) Ur-^{d}Šara

9) 6 úz-ama

10) 5 máš [šà-dùg]

Rev. 11) 2 u$_8$-ama

12) Ur-^{d}EN.ZU

(double line)

13) šu-nigín 83 udu

14) 2(DD) síg gú lá 4(||||) ma-na

15) 1(D) ì-nun dug 4(||||) sìlà

(space)

16) lá-ni 1(|) mu-a-kam

17) ^{d}Utu-mu-da

18) ì-da-gál

19) 25 mu 8 iti

35. (AO 11273)

Acquisition Genouillac, June 22, 1929. Light buff.
62 × 39 × 19 mm. Account of barley.

1) [10]+10 še gur-sag-gál-kug

2) GUR$_8$-gu-LUM

3) 6(gur) Ka-kug

4) 6(gur) Da-da dumu-kar

5) 5(gur) Barag-ga-ni lú-tir

6) 5(gur) Du-du KI.BE(⊳←)

7) 5(gur) KA-šè

8) 5(gur) Ur-é ugula-é

9) 5(gur) Lugal-DU(⊏⫣)

Rev. 10) 5(gur) Ur-lú lú-ŠIM+GAR

(space)

11) šu-nigín 52 še gur-sag-gál-kug

-25-

12) tir Ur-^{d}EN.ZU-ka-kam

13) ì-da$_x$(PI)-gál

   (space)

14) x mu x iti (under crystals)

36. (AO 11274)

Acquisition Genouillac, June 22, 1929. Buff-gray.
57 × 38 × 18 mm. Witnessed loan of silver. Plate IX.

1) 8 kug gí[n]

2) Lugal-KA-e

3) Ur-ki dumu Nin-ú-šè

4) ì-šè-lá

5) Nin-níg-zu

6) šu-du$_8$-a-bi (sic)

7) in-gub

8) 1 Ur-kun sipa

9) [1 $^{d?}$X-x-iš]?-da-[gal]

Rev. 10) 1 ^{d}Utu-gar

11) 1 Šeš-tur

12) 1 GIŠ.MI Du$_6$()-ba-al

13) 1 Ur-temen lú-ŠIM+GAR

14) 1 Inim-zi baḫar$_x$(wr. U.EDIN)

15) 1 Lugal-ab Bala-ki

16) 1 Šà-ga-ni dub-sar

17) lú-ki-inim-ma-me

37. (AO 11275)

Acquisition Genouillac, June 22, 1929. Light buff.
58 × 35 × 18 mm. Memo concerning the dwelling right

of a person and about his? commodities deposited with
two persons.   Plate X.

        1) 1 ^{d}ŠEŠ-sipa

        2) ^{d}ŠEŠ.KI-e-zu-a

        3) ì-tuš(⊟)

        4) dug₄-ga-ni

        5) ì-da-ti

            (double line)

        6) 1 urudu alal

        7) Lú-nigir-da

        8) ì-da-gál

        9) 3 še gur-sag-gál

Rev. 10) Ama-na-nam

       11) dam Lugal-níg-UL(⟨⊢⋈⟩)

       12) e-da-gál

            (double line)

       13) im GIŠ.MI-na-kam

(AO 11276, published by J. Nougayrol, "Conjuration
ancienne contre Samana," AOr XVII/2 [1949] 213-226
and plates III-IV)

38. (AO 11277)

Acquisition Genouillac, June 22, 1929. Light buff.
60 × 39 × 18 mm. Pointed forms of numbers in front
of (mu). Text similar to AO 11281. Account of
cattle.

        1) [x] áb-al

        2) [x] áb 3 (mu)

        3) [x] áb 2 (mu)

        4) 2 amar-gud 2 (mu)

        5) 3 amar da-ba

        6) Ur-^{d}Šara-kam

        7) 3 áb-al

        8) 1 áb 2 (mu)

        9) 3 amar da-ba

       10) Ur-^{d}EN.ZU-kam

Rev. 11) Ur-^{d}Nin-NAGAR.GÍD udul-da

       12) ì-da-sig$_7$
            (space)

       13) [x]+1 mu 4 iti

39. (AO 11278)

Acquisition Genouillac, June 22, 1929. Buff. 62 ×
37 × 17 mm. Account of threshed barley and emmer.
Plate X.

        1) 180+50+[x? še] gur-sag-g[ál]-dùl

        2) 10 zíz gur

        3) Ur-kud

        4) 203(gur) 2(pi) še gur

        5) Lugal-barag

        6) [60]+60+20(gur) 2(pi) še gur

        7) Lugal-AŠ(⸢ ⸣)-ni

        8) 148(gur) 2(pi) še ⸢gur⸣

        9) 4 zíz gur

       10) Ba-bi x (perhaps no sign)

       11) (space) or [zi-ga]

Rev.   (space)

       12) šu-nigín 600+120+1+[x še]
            gur-[sa]g-gá[l-dùl]

                    -28-

13) šu-nigín 12+[2 zíz gur]

14) še-giš-ra-a

15) sig₇ a-šà ^{d}En-l[íl-lá]

16) še-ḫal-bi íb-ta-zi

17) zíz-uš-bi šà-ba ì-gál

18) ugula Sag-du₅

(space)

19) 4 iti

40. (AO 11279)

Acquisition Genouillac, June 22, 1929. Light buff.
64 × 44 × 18 mm. Account of sheep and goats. Lines
19-21 reconstructed after AO 11292:16-18. Plate XI.

1) 7? u₈-ama

2) 2? SAL-sila₄ šà-dùg

3) 4? sila₄-nita šà-dùg

4) 46 ùz-ama

5) 6 SAL.SI.ÂŠ.GÀR šà-dùg

6) 7 máš-nita

(double line)

7) šu-nigín 72 udu-ùz gub-ba

8) Ur-^{dx}Šara-ka-kam

9) 5 u₈-ama

Rev. 10) 2 sila₄-nita šà-dùg

11) 31 ùz-ama

12) 7 SAL.SI.ÂŠ.GÀR šà-dùg

13) [20] (no space for 20 lá 1)

máš šà-dùg

(double line)

14) [šu-nigín 20]+44 udu-ùz gub-ba

15) [U]r-^{d}EN.ZU-ka-kam

16) 7 u$_8$-ama

17) 3 udu-nita 1 máš ùz-da

18) Lugal-KA-kam

19) lá-ni-bi bar-ta ⌈ba⌉-gál

20) ⌈zi⌉-zi-bi ì-ta-zi

L.E. 21) im-⌈si-sá-à⌉m

22) A-bí-⌈nar sipa⌉

R.E. 23) 4 mu 8 iti

41. (AO 11280)

Acquisition Genouillac, June 22, 1929. Light buff.
73 × 32 × 16 mm. Memo concerning various commodities
deposited by one person. Plate X.

1) 11 ì-erin UD.UD silà

2) 3 lá igi-4-gál ì-šim-tur-tur silà

3) 10 erin UD.UD ma-na

4) 10 še gur-sag-gál

5) 1 sum gur-sag-gál

6) 10 <ninda>? bappir

7) 10 bar-⌈si⌉ gada

8) 5 kuš UD.GA

Rev.   (space)

9) 1 ^{GIŠ}⌈šu⌉-kár šu-du$_7$-a gud-apin

10) Ama-é-e

11) Šà-da dub-sar-da

12) ì-da-tuku

42. (AO 11281)

Acquisition Genouillac, June 22, 1929. Light buff.
72 × 45 × 17 mm. Pointed forms of numbers in front
of (mu). Text similar to AO 11277. Account of
cattle.

1) 11 áb-ama
2) 1 áb 3 (mu)
3) 1 áb 2 (mu)
4) 1 gud 2 (mu)
5) 3 áb 1 (mu)
6) 1 gud 1 (mu)
   (double line)
7) šu-nigín 18 áb-amar
8) Ur-^{d}Šara-ka-kam
9) 3 áb-ama
10) 1 [....]
    (rest destroyed)

Rev.   (double line)
1') šu-nigín 10 áb-ama[r]
2') Ur-^{d}EN.ZU-ka-[kam]
3') ki Nir-d[a?-....]
4') Lugal-K[A-e]?
5') ì-[....]
6') Ur-^{d}[Nin-NAGAR.GÍD] ud[ul-da]
7') [ì-da-sig$_{7}$]
   (space)
8') 7 [mu x i]ti

43. (AO 11282)

Acquisition Genouillac, June 22, 1929. Dark gray, almost black. 46 × 31 × 16 mm. Issue of barley.

    1) 200 še gur-sag-gál-dùl

    2) Ama-barag

    3) 190 še gur

    4) Ur-ša$_6$-ga

    5) 190 še gur

    6) Al-la

    7) 184 še gur

Rev. 8) Mu-ni

      (space)

    9) šu-nigín 764 še gur-sag-gál-dùl

   10) še zi-ga

   11) Ur-ur

   12) sig$_7$ BAR.DU

   13) 5 mu 3 iti

44. (AO 11283)

Acquisition Genouillac, June 22, 1929. Light buff. 68 × 40 × 18 mm. Account of sheep and goats. Plate XII.

    1) 63 u$_8$-⟨ama⟩

    2) 20 udu-nita

    3) 7 sila$_4$-nita šà-dùg

    4) 10 SAL-sila$_4$ šà-dùg

    5) 53 ùz-ama

    6) 8 SAL.ÁŠ.GÀR šà-dùg

    7) 3 máš-sag

    8) 3 máš šà-dùg

9) Ur-^{d}Šara

10) 23 u$_{8}$-ama

Rev. 11) 6 udu-nita

12) 4 sila$_{4}$-nita šà-dùg

13) 6 SAL-sila$_{4}$ šà-dùg

14) 35 ùz-ama

15) 6 SAL.ÂŠ.GÀR šà-dùg

16) 4 máš-nita šà-dùg

17) Ur-^{d}EN.ZU

18) udu É.A-si$_{4}$-na

19) ^{d}Utu-mu-≪na≫-kam

20) Na-EŠ-dù-a ba-ur$_{4}$

21) ad-da-bi

22) ba-DU.DU

L.E. 23) 25 mu 8 iti

45. (AO 11284)

Acquisition Genouillac, June 22, 1929. Gray-buff.
66 × 46 × 20 mm. Account of barley.

1) 32?(gur) 3(pi) še gur-sag-gál

2) Nin-mes-e šu-ba-ti

3) 7 [še] gur

4) še anše-kú-a
(space)

5) 3(gur) 40(silà) še gur

6) gud-e-kú TÚG.ŠUM

7) A.LÙ.ZA

8) Lugal-tir

Rev. 9) [x(gur)] 20(silà) še gur

10) še gud-e-kú

-33-

11) TÚG.ŠUM A.LÙ.ZA

12) Ur-^{d}Nin-NAGAR.GÍD

46. (AO 11285)

Acquisition Genouillac, June 22, 1929. Light buff. 44 × 34 × 18 mm. Covered with salts; needs cleaning. Account of sheep and goats.

        1) 11 u_8-ama

        2) 20 lá 3 ùz-ama

        3) É-gud

        4) 1 u_8 8 ùz

        5) Igi-⌜nin⌝

        6) 2? u_8 x ùz

        7) ^{d}Utu-ḫi-li

        8) x u_8 3 ùz

Rev. 9) Nigín

      10) x u_8 x ùz

      11) ⌜Ur⌝-^{d}Utu

      12) x u_8 5 ùz

      13) ⌜Ur⌝-LI

47. (AO 11286)

Acquisition Genouillac, June 22, 1929. Light buff. 38 × 30 × 15 mm. Issue of flour. Plate XI.

        1) 40(silà) zíd

        2) Da-áš-lul

        3) 10(silà) Ab-kid(⊞)

        4) 30(silà) Ur-du_6

        5) 20(silà) Níg-du_8-du_8

Lo.E. 6) 10(silà) Na-na

Rev. 7) 10(silà) Um-mi-mi

8) 10(silà) DINGIR-ma-LÚ

(not DINGIR-ma ašgab)

9) 10(silà) Šeš-a

(double line)

10) šu-nigín 2(pi) 20(silà) zíd gur

11) zíd zi-ga

12) Šeš-a

48. (AO 11287)

Acquisition Genouillac, June 22, 1929. Dark gray.
76 × 42 × 18 mm. Account of threshed barley, emmer,
and wheat.

1) [1464(gur) 2(pi) še

gur-sag-gál-dùl]

2) 120+30+[17(gur) 2(pi) zíz gu]r

3) 11(gur) 2(pi) gig gur

4) Ur-^{d}Ab-ú

5) 1200+180+10(gur) 1(pi) 20(silà)

še gur

6) 20+[30] lá 2(gur) zíz gur

7) Sag-du$_5$

8) 600+420+5(gur) 1(pi) še gur

9) 16 zíz gur

10) Ur-dam

11) 240 lá 10(gur) še gur

12) Lugal-nagar-zi

Rev. (space)

13) šu-nigín 1 gur$_7$ 1200+310(gur) lá

40(silà) še gur-sag-gál-dùl

14) [šu-nigín] 180+51(gur) 2(pi) zíz
    gur

15) 11(gur) 2(pi) gig gur

16) še-giš-ra-a

17) sig$_7$ BAR.DU

49. (AO 11288)

Acquisition Genouillac, June 22, 1929. Light gray.
35 × 29 × 14 mm. Account of threshed barley.

1) 41 še gur-sag-gál

2) Ur-ab

3) 40 lá 2 še gur

4) Lugal-SAG

Rev. 5) še-giš-ra-a

6) sig$_7$ a-šà gibil

7) ugula Ur-dam
   (space)

8) 4 iti

50. (AO 11289)

Acquisition Genouillac, June 22, 1929. Light buff.
47 × 37 × 16 mm. Memo concerning various commodities
deposited with one person. Plate XII.

1) 1/2? kug m[a-na ....]

2) 1 níg-luḫ em[e?-....]

3) ki-lá-bi 2 ma-na 12 gín

4) 30 lá 2 udu-máš-ḫi-a

5) 1 má-gur$_8$ šu-du$_7$-a

6) 2 ^{GIŠ}umbin-UŠ

7) [x]+1 ^{GIŠ}umbin-mar

(rest destroyed)

Rev.　　(beginning destroyed)

1')　⌈Ur-mes⌉ sukal-da

2')　i-da-gál

51.　(AO 11290)

Acquisition Genouillac, June 22, 1929.　Gray.　46 ×
33 × 18 mm.　Witnessed contract concerning the purchase of an equid.　Plate XIII.

1)　1 anše-BAR.AN nita

2)　UŠ.KU dumu Lugal-kar-e-si
　　　lú-má-gur$_8$-ka-šè

3)　Lugal-KA-e

4)　i-šè-šám

5)　11 kug gín

6)　i-na-lá

Rev. 7)　[1 PN]

8)　[dumu PN]

9)　1 ⌈A⌉-bu-ḫa-DU

10)　dumu Ur-zu

11)　1 Lugal-níg-ba É/DAG.DÙG dam-gàr

12)　1 Ama-UM+ME.GA

13)　lú-ki-inim-ma-me

52.　(AO 11291)

Acquisition Genouillac, June 22, 1929.　Light buff.
40 × 31 × 16 mm.　Account of goats and sheep.

1)　lá-ni 5 máš

2)　3 u$_8$-ama

3)　2 udu-nita

-37-

4) Ur-^{d}Šara-ka-kam

5) lá-ni

6) ^{d}Utu-mu

Rev. 7) sipa-da

8) ì-da-sig$_7$

(space)

9) 4 mu 8 iti

53. (AO 11292)

Acquisition Genouillac, June 22, 1929. Light buff. 65 × 44 × 17 mm. For lines 16-18 cf. AO 11279: 19-21. Account of sheep and goats.

1) 13 u$_8$-ama

2) 3 udu-nita

3) 4 SAL-sila$_4$ šà-dùg

4) 40 lá 1 ùz-ama

5) 12 SAL.ÀŠ.GÀR šà-dùg

6) 1 máš šà-dùg

(double line)

7) šu-nigín 72 udu-ùz gub-ba

8) Ur-^{d}Šara-ka-kam

9) 6 u$_8$-ama

Rev. 10) 1 SAL-sila$_4$ šà-dùg

11) 40+[x ùz-a]ma

12) 4+[x SAL.ÀŠ.GÀR šà]-dùg

13) 1+[x máš šà]-dùg

(double line)

14) šu-[nigín x udu]-ùz [gub]-ba

15) U[r-^{d}EN.ZU]-ka-kam

16) lá-[ni-b]i bar-ta ⌈ba⌉-gál

-38-

17) zi-zi-ga-bi ì-ta-zi

18) im-si-sá-àm

19) A-bí-nar sipa

L.E. 20) 3 mu 8 iti

54. (AO 11293)

Acquisition Genouillac, June 22, 1929. Gray. 36 ×
27 × 15 mm. Memo concerning barley and emmer.

1) 220 še gur-sag-gál-si-sá

2) 140 lá 3 zíz gur-si-sá

3) Lú-^{d}Ba-ú-ke$_4$

4) Lugal-KA-ra

5) ì-na-bal

Rev.   (uninscribed)

55. (AO 11294)

Acquisition Genouillac, June 22, 1929. Gray. 43 ×
36 × 17 mm. Account of sheep.

1) 8 u$_8$-ama

2) 11 SAL-sila$_4$ šà-dùg

3) 3 SAL-sila$_4$ UD.DU-li

4) 14 udu-nita

5) udu ur$_4$-ra

6) É.A-si$_4$-na

Rev.   (uninscribed)

56. (AO 11295)

Acquisition Genouillac, June 22, 1929. Light buff.
66 × 52 × 22 mm. Account of sheep and goats. Plate
XIII.

-39-

1) 13 udu-nita
2) 10 u$_8$-ama
3) 16 sila$_4$ ša-dùg
4) 4 ùz
5) 4 máš ša-dùg
6) 1 máš-gal
(double line)
7) šu-nigín 46 udu-ḫi-a
8) lá-ni 2 [udu-ḫi-a]
9) [....]

Rev. 10) [...]x-ma-⌈sur-ra⌉
11) [....-t]a-⌈x⌉-ta-ra-a
12) ⌈X⌉(🌲)-ma í-lá
13) udu zi-ga kuš zag-šuš kuš
    nu-šuš dù-a-bi íb-[t]a-zi
14) Ur-^{d}[ŠE.T]IR?(𒀀) KA.SAR.RA
15) níg-ŠID-bi í-ag
16) 16 mu 7 iti til-la

57. (AO 11296)

Acquisition Genouillac, June 22, 1929. Gray. 66 ×
37 × 17 mm. Account of threshed barley and emmer.

1) 6 še gur-sag-gál-dùl
2) Lugal-KA
3) 71 še gur
4) Lugal-TUR.ŠÈ
5) 66 še gur
6) Nigìn
7) 173 še gur
8) Ur-ša$_6$

9) 600+60+40(gur) še 8(gur) zíz gur

10) Si-dù

11) 281 še gur

Rev. 12) Lugal-nagar-zi

13) sig₇ a-šà ^{d}En-líl-lá

14) 130 še gur

15) Ne-sag

16) 60 še gur

17) UŠ.KU sipa

18) sig₇ a-šà ^{d}Innin

19) še-giš-ra-a

20) BAR.DU

(space)

21) [x]+3 iti

58. (AO 11297)

Acquisition Genouillac, June 22, 1929. Light buff.
66 × 38 × 17 **mm**. Account of goats and sheep.

1) lá-ni 10 ùz-ama

2) 7 máš-nita

(double line)

3) šu-nigín 20 lá 3 ùz

4) Ur-^{d}Šara-ka-kam

5) 4 ùz-ama

6) 1 máš-nita

7) Ur-^{d}EN₀ZU-kam

8) lá-ni

Rev. 9) ^{d}Utu-mu sipa-

10) da-kam

(space)

-41-

11) 6 mu 3 iti

59. (AO 11298)

Acquisition Genouillac, June 22, 1929. Light buff.
48 × 34 × 16 mm. Account of sheep and goats. Plate
XIII.

1) lá 3 u$_8$-ama

2) 2 udu-nita

3) 2 SAL-sila$_4$ šà-dùg

4) 12 máš

(double line)

5) šu-nigín 20 lá 2 udu lá-ni

6) Ur-^{dx}Sara-ka-kam

Rev. 7) A-bí-nar sipa

(space)

8) 2 mu 8 iti

60. (AO 11299)

Acquisition Genouillac, June 22, 1929. Light buff.
44 × 34 × 17 mm. Pointed forms of numbers in front
of (mu). Text not finished. Account of sheep.

1) 600 udu-sukkal 3 (mu)

2) UN-íl dím

3) Lugal-šu-maḫ sipa

4) 480 udu AŠ(٤).RU 3 (mu)

(rest uninscribed)

Rev.   (uninscribed)

61. (AO 11300)

Acquisition Genouillac, June 22, 1929. Light buff.

46 × 34 × 14 mm. Account of goatskins, goats, and
sheep.

        1) 2 kuš ùz zag-šuš

        2) 1 máš nu-šuš

        3) Ur-^{d}Šara-ka-kam

        4) 1 máš Ur-^{d}Šara dub-sar

        5) 1 ùz zag-šuš

        6) Si-dù sipa

        7) Ur-^{d}EN.ZU

Rev. 8) 1 kuš ùz

        9) 1 kuš máš zag-šuš

     10) 1 udu-nita zag-šuš

     11) 1 sila$_4$ zag-šuš

     12) ^{d}Utu-mu sipa

     13) Na-EŠ-dù-a

     14) 5 mu 4 iti

62. (AO 11301)

Acquisition Genouillac, June 22, 1929. Gray-buff.
41 × 32 × 14 mm. Pointed forms of numbers. Account
of threshed barley.

        1) 10 še gur-sag-gál

        2) Lugal-KA

        3) 10 Lugal-TUR.ŠÈ

        4) 10 Nigìn

        5) še-giš-ra-a

        6) sig$_7$ A.LÙ.ZA

Rev. 7) ugula Lugal-KA

        8) má dub-sag

        (space)

9) 16 mu 4 iti

63. (AO 11302)

Acquisition Genouillac, June 22, 1929. Light buff.
47 × 33 × 16 mm. Account of goatskins and sheepskins.
1) 6 kuš ùz zag-šuš
2) 3 kuš ùz zag-nu-šuš
3) 1 kuš u₈ zag-šuš
4) Ur-ᵈEN.ZU-kam
Rev.   (uninscribed)

64. (AO 11303)

Acquisition Genouillac, June 22, 1929. Buff to gray.
66 × 45 × 21 mm. A parallel text in AO 11308. Memo
concerning various commodities deposited with one
person. Plate XIV.
1) [20 lá 1 še gur-sag]-gál
2) [2] urudu UD.KA-bar
3) [1] túg ti(sic, cf. AO 11308)
4) [1] túg TUM.BA.DÙ
5) [1] túg ŠÀ.GI.URUDU
6) [2] túg gú-anše
7) [2] barag gibil
8) [10]+2 kuš UD.G[A]
9) [2] kuš A.EDIN.N[A] (sic,
     apparently not L[Á])
10) [1] kuš ANŠE.ED[IN]
Rev. 11) [30 lá 1 giš-ùr]
12) [120] gi sa mes

-44-

13) 1 $^{GI\check{S}}$KA.UMBIN(⟨cuneiform signs⟩)

14) 1 SAL$_4$(QA).SA.KA (cf. AO 11308)

15) Da-⌈ša$_6$⌉

16) i-da-[gá]l

65. (AO 11304)

Acquisition Genouillac, June 22, 1929. Buff to gray.
44 × 33 × 20 mm. Note concerning the purchase of a
house. Plate XIV.

1) 4 kug gín

2) ši$_4$-bi-ir-tum é-kam

3) Ama-é dam Ur-^{d}Šara-ka-⌈ke$_4$⌉

4) Ur-mes

5) dumu Du-du-ra

Rev. 6) i-na-lá

66. (AO 11305)

Acquisition Genouillac, June 22, 1929. Gray. 59 ×
37 × 17 mm. Account of threshed barley.

1) 61 še gur-sag-gál-dùl

2) É-e

3) 16(gur) 2(pi) še gur

4) A-kal-li

5) 47 še gur

6) Ur-^{d}TUR

7) ugula É-e

8) 61(gur) 1(pi) še gur

9) Lugal-še

10) [x še] gur

11) [PN]

Rev. 12) [x]+22 še gur

13) ⌜U⌝r-^{GIŠ}gigir

14) [u]gula Lugal-še

15) še-giš-ra-a

16) sig$_7$ a-šà gibil

17) du$_6$ NISABA(inversum)^{SAR}

(space)

18) 4 (or ⌜5⌝) iti

67. (AO 11306)

Acquisition Genouillac, June 22, 1929. Gray. 44 ×
32 × 15 mm. Account of threshed barley, emmer, and
wheat.

1) 360+24 še gur-sag-gál

2) 52 ziz gur

3) ⌜4⌝ gig gur

4) sig$_7$ A.LÙ.ZA

5) 180+22(gur) 2(pi) še gur

6) sig$_7$ a-šà ^{d}Nin-tu

7) 45(gur) 2(pi) še gur

Rev. 8) sig$_7$ a-šà ^{d}En-líl-lá

(double line)

9) šu-nigin 600+32 še gur-sag-gál

10) šu-nigin 52 ziz gur

11) [šu-nigin 4 gi]g gur

12) še-[giš-r]a-a

13) Lugal-KA

68. (AO 11307)

Acquisition Genouillac, June 22, 1929. Light buff.

50 × 36 × 15 mm. Witnessed memo concerning two amounts
of silver deposited by two persons with one person.
Plate XIV.

1) 8 kug gín
2) Kud-du UŠ-a-bi
3) 4 kug gín
4) Ama-[é-e]
5) Ì-li
6) dam DINGIR-an-dùl-da
7) ì-da-tuku
8) A-[....]
9) Lugal-an-[ni]?
Rev. 10) dumu Ur-^{d}EN.ZU
11) Lugal-KA-gu-la
12) lú-ki-inim-ma-bi-me
13) u(d)-ba En-an-na-DU
14) en$_{5}$-si Umma^{KI}

69. (AO 11308)

Acquisition Genouillac, June 22, 1929. Light buff.
68 × 48 × 19 mm. A parallel text in AO 11303. Memo
concerning various commodities deposited with one
person. Plate XV.

1) 20 lá 1 še gur-sag-gál
2) 2 urudu UD.KA-bar
3) 1 túg bal(sic, cf. AO 11303)
4) 1 túg TUM.BA.DÙ
5) 1 túg ŠÀ.GI.URUDU
6) 2 túg gú-anše
7) 2 barag gibil

-47-

8) 12 kuš UD.GA

9) 2 kuš A.EDIN

10) 1 kuš ANŠE.EDIN

11) 30 lá 1 giš-ùr

Rev. 12) 120 gi sa mes

13) 1 GIŠ.KA.UMBIN(⟨ꗠ— ꖼ⟩)

14) 1 SAL(sic).SA.[KA] (cf. AO 11303)

15) Da-[ša₆]

16) ì-da-gál

70. (AO 11309)

Acquisition Genouillac, June 22, 1929. Buff-gray.
58 × 40 × 18 mm. Witnessed memo concerning the issue
of oil and grain as provisions for a person. Plate
XVI.

1) 2(gur) 10(silà) ì-kal-silà

2) 2 1/2 kug gín-[bi]

3) 50(silà) ŠE.MUŠ

4) níg-kú-a

5) ᵈEn-líl-li-kam

6) é Zag-mu-ta (or é zag-mu-ta)

7) AN a-ta è

(space)

Rev. 8) 1 Lugal-ša₆

9) dumu Ur-PA

10) 1 Bar-ra-ni-še

11) dumu MES-kisal-li

12) 1 Ur-ZU.AB GAL.NI

13) 1 Ka-kug ugula uru

14) 1 A-ba-an-da-di

15) dumu Kum-ku-šè

16) lú-ki-inim-ma-bi-me

L.E. 17) Inim-ma-ni maškim

71. (AO 11310)

Acquisition Genouillac, June 22, 1929. Buff-gray. 64 × 40 × 18 mm. Memo concerning four items (two objects, silver, a sheep) and a loan. Plate XV.

1) <1> NUMUN-ša$_6$-ga

2) 3 kug gín-kam

3) ḫa-zi-gú-bir$_5$-ka

4) ab-gar

5) 1 GUR$_8$.GUR$_8$ bal-a urudu

6) 5 kug gín-kam

7) sag Lú-giš-šè

8) Lugal-⌈sár?-ra⌉? ba-DU

9) 1 kug gín Ur-gu

10) nu-banda ba-DU

11) 1 udu-nita

12) [kug ig]i-4-gál-kam

Rev.   (erasure)

13) [L]ú-giš-e ba-DU

14) [L]ú-giš dumu Lú-barag-[g]i-da

15) [L]ú-na-nam simug

16) an-da-tuku

17) 16 še gur-sag

18) é Lugal-KA-šè simug-ta

19) dam É-da-lu MU-ke$_4$

20) ḪAR-šè šu-ba-ti

21) nu-SU

-49-

72. (AO 11311)

Acquisition Genouillac, June 22, 1929. Buff-gray.
67 × 38 × 17 mm. Pointed forms of numbers. 60 gur
is written horizontally; units for 1-9 gur are
written vertically (slightly slanted). Account of
threshed barley and emmer.

1) [x] lá 1 še g[ur-sa]g-gál-[dù1]?
2) [x] zíz gur
3) [D]a?-da
4) 74(gur) 𓀭 še gur
5) UŠ.KU
6) 82 še gur
7) Ur-ab
8) 80 lá 2 še gur
9) Lugal-SAG
10) 76 še gur
11) Ur-d[a]?
12) [še-g]iš-ra-[a]

Rev. 13) sig₇ BAR.DU
14) UŠ.KU šu-i(𓏤)
15) šu-ba-ti

73. (AO 11312)

Acquisition Genouillac, June 22, 1929. Gray. 69 ×
36 × 15 mm. Memo concerning the deposition of silver
and barley with one person. Plate XVII.

1) 10 l[á 1 kug gín]
2) 1 še gur-sag-gál
3) Ama-še-numun-zi
4) 1 kug (gín) Úr-kug-gi

         5) 1 kug (gín) ME-nigìn

         6) šu-nigìn 11 kug gín

         7) 1 še gur-sag-gál

         8) Ama-é-da

         9) ì-da-tuku

        10) 1 kug gín

Rev. 11) Ur-^dNin-NAGAR.GÍD sipa

        12) 2 kug gín É-úr

        13) ad-kub_x

        14) 1 kug gín Da-bu-a

        15) 1 [kug gín Lu]gal-e

        16) 1 [kug gín X]-du (⬭⬭)

        17) 1 kug [gín] Ur-mes zadim

        18) 1 kug gín Šu-me

        19) Ama-⌈é⌉-e (sic) ì-da_x(PI)-tuku

                74. (AO 11313)

Acquisition Genouillac, June 22, 1929. Buff-gray.
80 × 46 × 18 mm. Pointed forms of numbers. 60 gur
is written horizontally; units for 1-9 gur are
written vertically (slightly slanted). Account of
threshed barley.

         1) [x] še gur-[sa]g-gál

         2) [Lugal]-ab

         3) 71(gur) ⚟ še gur

         4) Du-du

         5) 70 lá 2 še gur

         6) Ba-za

         7) 70(gur) ⚟ še gur

         8) UŠ.KU dumu Da-da
                        -51-

(double line)

9) še-giš-ra-a

10) Ur-PA dub-sar

11) sig₇ BAR.DU

Rev.   (uninscribed)

75.   (AO 11314)

Acquisition Genouillac, June 22, 1929. Light buff.
68 × 55 × 24 mm. Pointed forms of numbers in lines
9 and 15. Account of sheep and goats.

1) 71 u$_8$-[am]a

2) 15 SAL-sila$_4$ šà-dùg

3) 56 udu-nita

4) 30 lá 1 ùz-ama

5) 5 SAL.ÁŠ.GÀR šà-dug 5(𒀹)

6) 13 máš-nita

(double line)

7) šu-nigín 142 udu

8) šu-nigín 50 lá 3 ùz

9) lá-ni 5 u$_8$ 8 udu-nita 2 ùz

Rev. 10) lá-ni-àm šà-ba ì-šid

11) udu zi-ga íb-ta-zi

12) im-si-sá-àm

13) udu Ur-^{d}Šara-ka-kam

14) En-an-ni e-da-sig₇

15) 16 SAL-sila$_4$ 16 sila$_4$ 6 SAL.ÁŠ.GÀR
      4 máš šà-dùg mu-a-kam

16) En-an-ni sag udu-gal-gal-šè

17) šà udu-ka MI ì-⌈gi$_4$⌉(𒀹)

18) 15 mu 7 iti še-ba ŠE.KIN.T[AR]?

( )

19) A.LÙ.ZA-ka ba-ur$_4$

76. (AO 11315)

Acquisition Genouillac, June 22, 1929. Light buff. 66 × 60 × 17 mm. Two-column text. Account of sheep and goats.

i 1) 11 u$_8$-ama

2) 3 SAL-sila$_4$ ša-dùg

3) 3 ⌈sila⌉-nita$_4$ ša-dùg

4) 34 ùz-ama

5) 15 SAL.SI.ÁŠ.GÀR

6) 3 máš ša-dúg

(double line)

7) šu-nigín 70 lá ùz-udu

8) Ur-^{d}Šara-ka-kam

ii 1) 26 ùz-ama

2) 13 SAL.SI.ÁŠ.GÀR ša-dùg

3) 2 máš ša-dùg

4) 7 u$_8$-ama

5) 2 SAL-sila$_4$ ša-dùg

6) 1 sila$_4$-nita ša-dùg

(double line)

7) šu-nigín 51 ùz-udu

8) Ur-^{d}EN.ZU-ka-kam

Rev. i 1) udu gub-ba É.A-si$_4$-na

2) A-bí-nar sipa-

3) da ì-da-sig$_7$

4) Ur-sipa-da sipa

-53-

5) na-gada (cf. AO 11267)

ii 1) 2 mu 8 iti

77. (AO 11316)

Acquisition Genouillac, June 22, 1929. Gray-black.
75 × 48 × 21 mm. Witnessed contract concerning the
purchase of a person. Plate XVIII.

1) 10 lá 1 kug gín
2) níg-šám+àm
3) Nin-maš-e GAR (wr. 𒑱)
4) Nin-maš-e
5) Nin-pàd-da ama-ni
6) šu-ne-ne ab-si
7) Inim-ma-ni
8) ì-ne-lá
9) giš-gan-na ab-ta-bal
10) ì sag-šè sag-bi a ba-sum

Rev. 11) Nin-pàd-da
12) lú-níg-[šám-k]ú-àm
13) Inim-[ma-ni]
14) lú-[níg-šám-ag-àm]
(double line)
15) 1 ^{d}[...]
16) dumu [....]
17) 1 [....]
18) dumu [....]
19) 1 Ú[r?-ni? a]šgab?
20) dumu Tir?-kug sipa
21) 1 ^{d}En-líl-li

22) dumu Ka-kug ugula udul

L.E. 23) lú-ki-inim-ma-bi-me

78. (AO 11317)

Acquisition Genouillac, June 22, 1929. Gray-black.
66 × 42 × 20 mm. Witnessed contract concerning the
purchase of a person. Plate XIX.

1) 6 kug gín

2) níg-ŠÁM+A Ki-sar-šè

3) É-kalam-e

4) Sag-^dEn-líl-da

5) dumu-ni

6) šu-ne-ne ab-si

7) Inim-ma-ni

8) ì-ne-lá

9) 1 Lugal-túg-maḫ(𒍠)

Rev. 10) IGI.DU GAL.NI

11) 1 Lugal-giš

12) dumu Li-li

13) 1 Lugal-engar-dùg dam-⌈gàr⌉

14) 1 Zag-mu [...].

15) 1 Ur-ša₆-[ga]

16) 1 Lugal-uku-⌈gá⌉

17) dumu ⌈U⌉r-éš-⌈líl⌉

18) 1 É-EZEN-ri-e

19) UŠ.KU

L.E. 20) lú-ki-inim-ma-bi-me

79. (AO 11318)

Acquisition Genouillac, June 22, 1929. Light buff.

50 × 34 × 18 mm. Pointed forms of numbers. Account
of goats, sheep, and goatskins.

          1)   2 máš

          2)   1 ùz-ama

          3)   Ur-^{d}Utu sipa

          4)   1 u_8-ama

          5)   1 udu-nita

          6) ^{d}Dumu-zi-an-dùl ba-DU.DU

          7)   Ur-^{d}Šara-ka-kam

          8)   2 máš

          9)   Lu-lu

Rev. 10)   1 máš zag-nu-šuš

         11)   ⌈A⌉-bu-ḫa-DU

         12)   2 kuš ùz-ama

         13) ^{d}Utu-mu sipa mu-DU

         14)   zi-zi-ga-àm

            (space)

         15)   7 mu 8 iti

           80.   (AO 11319)

Acquisition Genouillac, June 22, 1929. Buff-gray.
54 × 41 × 20 mm. Witnessed contract concerning the
purchase of a person. Plate XX.

          1)   5 kug gín

          2)   níg-šám

          3)   Á-ni-ta

          4)   KA(clear) Ur-^{d}Innin

          5) ^{d}En-líl-dingir-zu

          6)   dumu Ka-kug

          7)   ba-DU

Rev. 8) 1 Ur-^{d}Da-mu

9) uku-uš ugula-é

10) maškim ⌈di⌉ si-sá-a-bi

11) 1 Ur-^{d}IM

12) 1 Mes-ZU.AB

13) 1 Lugal-šà

14) 1 Ur-mes 🔲🔳

15) 1 ^{d}En-líl-🔲🔳

L.E. 16) lú-ki-inim-ma-bi

81. (AO 11320)

Acquisition Genouillac, June 22, 1929. Buff-gray;
originally brown, parts became gray after a fire.
64 × 50 × 24 mm. Witnessed contract concerning the
purchase of a person. Plate XVII.

1) 6 kug gín

2) níg-ŠÁM+A Zag-mu [GAR]

3) kug 🔷🔷   TUR 🔲[....]

4) Zag-m[u dumu] ⌈A⌉-zu-[zu]

5) Nin-níg-x(🔲)-e ama-n[i]

6) šu-ne-ne a[b-si]

7) Inim-ma-ni lú-níg-[ŠÁM+A-ag-àm]

8) Nin-níg-x(🔲)-e lú-níg-
    [ŠÁM+A]-kú-à[m]

    (double line)

9) 1 Ur-ša₆-⌈ga⌉

Rev. 10) lú Ur-^{d}šara

11) 1 Da-ša₆

12) 1 Ne-sag

13) dumu Me-lám-an-ni-[m]e

-57-

14) 1 Ur-^{d}Dumu-zi-da

15) 1 Lú-ti-dingir-zu

16) dumu Ka-kug-me

(space)

17) lú-ki-inim-ma-bi-me

82. (AO 11321)

Acquisition Genouillac, June 22, 1929. Light buff. 30 × 27 × 15 mm. Pointed forms of numbers. Account of goats.

1) 1 ùz-ama

2) 1 máš zag-šuš

3) 1 máš šà-dùg

4) Ur-^{dx}Sara-ka-kam

Lo.E. 5) ^{d}Utu-mu-gi$_4$ sipa

Rev. 6) Ezen-^{d}Dumu-zi-ka (wr. Ezen-

DUMU.AN.ZI.KA)

7) ì-DU

(space)

8) 5 mu

83. (AO 11322)

Acquisition Genouillac, June 22, 1929. Light buff. 28 × 24 × 15 mm. Account of goatskins.

1) 1 kuš ùz-ama

2) Ur-^{dx}Sara-ka-kam

3) 1 kuš ùz-ama

4) Ur-^{d}EN.ZU-kam

5) ^{d}Dumu-zi-an-dùl-e

Rev. 6) mu-DU

7) ^dUtu-mu sipa

(space)

8) 5 mu 10 lá 1 iti

84. (AO 11323)

Acquisition Genouillac, June 22, 1929. Gray-buff.
25 × 23 × 17 mm. Account of sheepskins.

1) 1 kuš u$_8$

2) 1 kuš udu-nita

3) Na-EŠ-dù-a^{KI}

4) En-za-bar-e

Rev. 5) mu-DU

(space)

6) 25 mu 10 lá 1 iti

85. (AO 11324)

Acquisition Genouillac, June 22, 1929. Gray. 20 ×
17 × 12 mm. Pointed forms of numbers. Account of
threshed barley.

1) 25(gur) še-ḫal-la gur-sag-gál

2) [U]r-dam

3) še-giš-ra-a

4) sig$_7$ BAR.DU

Rev. 5) UŠ.⌈KU⌉ šu-i(𒃶)

6) šu-ba-ti

86. (AO 11325)

Acquisition Genouillac, June 22, 1929. Gray. 27 ×
23 × 16 mm. Account of barley.

1) 180+43 še gur-sag-gál-dùl

2) En-šagana(ANŠE) sag-apin

3) gud ^{d}Šara

Rev.   (uninscribed)

87. (AO 11326)

Acquisition Genouillac, June 22, 1929. Light buff.
25 × 24 × 16 mm. Account of unusual kinds of goats.

1) 2 máš ḪIR.ḪIR.DU

2) 1 máš A.LÁ.A

3) Ur-^{d}EN.ZU ba-BE($\bowtie$)-a

Lo.E. 4) ba-zi

Rev. 5) máš Ur-^{d}Šara-ka-kam

(space)

6) 23 mu 8 iti

88. (AO 11327)

Acquisition Genouillac, June 22, 1929. Light buff.
25 × 20 × 15 mm. Account of one sheepskin.

1) 1 kuš u$_{8}$

2) ^{d}ZA.GÁR-dug$_{4}$-ga-ka

3) UŠ.KU-tur-e

4) Ur-^{d}EN.ZU-ra

Lo.E. 5) ì-na-gíd

Rev. 6) Ur-^{d}EN.ZU

(space)

7) 22 mu 10 lá 1 iti

89. (AO 11328)

Acquisition Genouillac, June 22, 1929. Light buff.
28 × 22 × 14 mm. Account of sheep and goats.

-60-

        1) 1 udu-nita
        2) A-a-<bi>-nar-e
        3) É.A-maš-zu-ta
        4) mu-DU
Lo.E. 5) 1 máš-nita
Rev. 6) 1 udu-nita
        7) udu A-bí-GI$_4$
        8) 22 mu 10 iti

                90. (AO 11329)
Acquisition Genouillac, June 22, 1929. Gray. 28 ×
26 × 14 mm. Account of threshed barley.
        1) 10(gur) lá 1(pi) še
                gur-sag-gál-dùl
        2) še-giš-ra-a
        3) Ur-igi
        4) sig$_7$ Amar-ú-ga
Rev.   (uninscribed)

                91. (AO 11330)
Acquisition Genouillac, June 22, 1929. Gray. 27 ×
24 × 13 mm. Pointed forms of numbers. Account of
threshed barley.
        1) 60+20+4(gur) še-ḫal-la
                gur-sag-gál
        2) še-giš-ra-a
        3) sig$_7$ BAR.DU
        4) UŠ.KU šu-i(𝍦)
Rev. 5) šu-ba-ti

                -61-

92. (AO 11331)

Acquisition Genouillac, June 22, 1929. Light buff.
31 × 26 × 14 mm. Account of one goatskin.

    1) 1(∇) kuš ùz zag-šuš

    2) Ur-zu-kam

    3) ^{d}Utu-mu-gi$_4$

    4) sipa

    (space)

    5) 4 mu 10 iti

Rev. (uninscribed)

93. (AO 11332)

Acquisition Genouillac, June 22, 1929. Buff-gray.
27 × 22 × 14 mm. Line 8 appears to be added after
the text had been completed with the date. Account
of goatskins.

    1) 1($\triangleright$) kuš ùz

    2) Lugal-e-gi

    3) nag-kud

    4) Inim-ma-ni-zi-da-šè

    5) mu-gíd

Rev. 6) Ur-^{d}šara

    (space)

    7) 23 mu 4 iti

    (space)

    8) 1(∇) kuš máš šà-dùg AN.A (⸝ ⸝)

94. (AO 11333)

Acquisition Genouillac, June 22, 1929. Light buff.
32 × 27 × 14 mm. Account of goats and sheep.

1) 3 máš zag-nu-šuš

2) 1 sila$_4$-nita

3) Ur-^{d}Šara-kam

4) 1 máš zag-nu-šuš

Rev. 5) Ur-^{d}EN.ZU-kam

6) máš zi-ga

7) ^{d}Utu-mu sipa

(space)

8) 5 mu 8 iti

95. (AO 11334)

Acquisition Genouillac, June 22, 1929. Light buff. 32 × 27 × 14 mm. Account of one goatskin.

1) 1 kuš ùz zag-šuš

2) Ur-^{d}Šara-ka-kam

3) ^{d}Utu-mu-gi$_4$ sipa

(space)

4) 4 mu 11 iti

Rev. (uninscribed)

96. (AO 11335)

Acquisition Genouillac, June 22, 1929. Light buff. 23 × 22 × 13 mm. Account of one goatskin.

1) 1 kuš ùz

2) Ur-^{d}EN.ZU-kam

3) A-bí-nar-e sipa

Rev. 4) AN.KI.KI-šè

5) Ezen-MURUB$_4$()-ka

6) mu-gíd

7) 5 mu 4 iti

97. (AO 11336)

Acquisition Genouillac, June 22, 1929. Light buff.
25 × 23 × 12 mm. Account of threshed barley, emmer,
and wheat.

  1) 40 še gur-sag-gál
  2) 15 zíz \<gur\>
Rev. 3) 7(gur) 2(pi) gig gur
  4) še-giš-ra-a
  5) a-šà gán-gíd-a
L.E. 6) A-du ba-ag
R.E. 7) 4 mu 5 iti

98. (AO 11337)

Acquisition Genouillac, June 22, 1929. Light buff.
26 × 22 × 13 mm. Account of one sheep. Plate XVIII.

  1) 1 udu-nita
  2) A-a-bí-nar-e
  3) pisan-udu-ta
  4) mu-DU
  5) uru-a ba-tag
Rev. 6) Ur-^{d}šara
  (space)
  7) 23 mu 3 iti

99. (AO 11338)

Acquisition Genouillac, June 22, 1929. Light buff.
25 × 22 × 14 mm. Account of one sheepskin.

  1) 1 kuš u$_8$
  2) nag-kud Inim-ma-ni-zi-da-ka
  3) Lugal-e-gi

Rev. 4)   mu-gíd

5)   Ur-^{d}šara

6)   23 mu 3 iti

100. (AO 11339)

Acquisition Genouillac, June 22, 1929. Light buff.
28 × 23 × 14 mm. Account of goatskins.

1)   2 ⌈kuš⌉ ùz

2)   Ur-^{d}šara-ka-kam

3)   1 kuš u$_8$

4)   Lugal-KA-kam

5)   2 kuš ùz

Rev. 6)   Ur-^{d}EN.ZU-ka-kam

7) ^{d}Utu-mu sipa-

8)   dè mu-DU

9)   4 mu 12 iti

101. (AO 11340)

Acquisition Genouillac, June 22, 1929. Light buff.
27 × 25 × 13 mm. Issue of barley.

1)   1 še gur-sag-gál-si-sá

2)   Ur-zu

3)   še zi-ga

4)   DINGIR-ga-lí

Rev.   (space)

5)   6 mu 7 iti

102. (AO 11341)

Acquisition Genouillac, June 22, 1929. Light buff.
25 × 23 × 14 mm. Account of one goatskin.

-65-

1) 1 kuš ùz

2) Ur-^dEN.ZU-kam

3) A-bí-nar-e

4) Lugal-KA-ra

Rev. 5) ì-na-gíd

(space)

6) 3 mu 10 lá 1 iti

103. (AO 11342)

Acquisition Genouillac, June 22, 1929. Gray. 28 ×
25 × 14 mm. Account of threshed barley.

1) 63 še gur-sag-gál

2) Ur-A.LÙ.ZA

3) še-giš-ra-a

4) sig$_7$ a-šà ^{<d>}En-líl-lá

Rev. 5) Lugal-KA

6) šu-ba-ti

7) ugula Ra-bal (clear)

8) 4 iti

104. (AO 11343)

Acquisition Genouillac, June 22, 1929. Gray. 28 ×
26 × 14 mm. Receipt of barley and emmer.

1) 100 lá 1 (gur) še

gur-sag-gál-dùl

2) 5 zíz gur

3) še Lugal-tar-kam

4) Lugal-KA-e

Rev. 5) šu-ba-ti

6) UŠ.KU dub-sar

        7) É-gal baḫar(EDIN)
        8) [x]+6 mu 6 iti

                105. (AO 11344)
Acquisition Genouillac, June 22, 1929。 Gray.   30 ×
24 × 14 mm。 Memo concerning grain placed in two
storehouses.
        1) 360+20 [še] gur-sag-gál
        2) é-DUB ⌈gu⌉-la-a
        3) ì-⌈si⌉
        4) 95 še gur-sag-gál
        5) é-DUB ⌈tur⌉-a
        6) ì-si

                106. (AO 11345)
Acquisition Genouillac, June 22, 1929. Light buff.
27 × 24 × 13 mm. Account of three sheep.
        1) 3 u_8
        2) A-a-bí-nar
        3) a-šà Ur-sag-pa-è-ta
  Rev. 4) mu-DU
        (space)
        5) 25 mu 12 iti

                107。 (AO 11346)
Acquisition Genouillac, June 22, 1929. Light buff.
29 × 26 × 13 mm. Account of two goats.
        1) 2 máš
        2) A-bí-nar-da
        3) sanga ba-da-ag
                -67-

Rev. 4) Bar-bi ba-DU.DU

(space)

5) 3 mu 8 iti

108. (AO 11347)

Acquisition Genouillac, June 22, 1929. Gray. 32 × 27 × 16 mm. Account of threshed barley.

1) 600+360+11 še gur-sag-gál-si-sá

2) Ur-^dKi-nà(d)

3) še-giš-ra-a

4) sig₇ BAR.DU

Rev. 5) Lugal-KA-e

6) šu-ba-ti

109. (AO 11348)

Acquisition Genouillac, June 22, 1929. Light buff. 26 × 25 × 13 mm. Account of one goatskin.

1) 1(⎾) kuš ùz zag-šuš

2) Ur-zu-kam

3) ^dUtu-mu sipa

(space)

4) 4 mu 11 iti

Rev. (uninscribed)

110. (AO 11349)

Acquisition Genouillac, June 22, 1929. Gray. 22 × 20 × 11 mm. Account of (threshed) emmer.

1) 3(gur) 2(pi) ziz gur-sag-gál

2) Ur-kud

3) sig₇ a-šà ^dEn-líl-lá-⌈kam⌉

Rev.   (uninscribed)

111. (AO 11350)

Acquisition Genouillac, June 22, 1929. Light buff.
32 × 25 × 13 mm. Account of sheepskins and goatskins.

1) 2 kuš u$_8$
2) 1 kuš ùz
3) Ur-^{d}Šara
4) 1 kuš ùz
5) Ur-^{d}EN.ZU
6) Lugal-e-gi

Rev. 7) ki GUR$_8$-gu-LUM-ma-šè
8) mu-gíd
   (space)
9) 22 mu 12 iti til-la

112. (AO 11351)

Acquisition Genouillac, June 22, 1929. Dark gray.
27 × 25 × 13 mm. Account of threshed barley and
emmer.

1) 286(gur) 1(pi) 30(silà)
   še gur-sag-gál
2) 10(gur) 2(pi) 30(silà) zíz gur
3) Ur-ša$_6$

Rev. 4) še-gi[š-ra-a]
5) sig$_7$ a-š[à ^{d}En-líl-lá]
   (space)
6) [x mu x] [iti]

113. (AO 11352)

Acquisition Genouillac, June 22, 1929. Light buff.
30 × 27 × 14 mm. Account of goatskins.

1) 4 kuš uz zag-šuš
2) 2 kuš uz zag-nu-šuš
3) en₅-si ŠUKU.ᵈINNIN-ka

Rev. 4) mu ti-la-a
5) ᵈDumu-zi-an-dùl-e
6) mu-DU
7) 3 mu 10 iti

114. (AO 11353)

Acquisition Genouillac, June 22, 1929. Buff-gray.
29 × 23 × 15 mm. Account of one goatskin.

1) 1 kuš uz
2) su₇ Uš-su-da
3) ba-a-BE
4) A-ḫu-ḫu-e
5) A-sar-AN.TI.LA-šè

Rev. 6) šu-e im-mi-uš
7) Ur-ᵈŠara
(space)
8) 23 mu 2 iti

115. (AO 11354)

Acquisition Genouillac, June 22, 1929. Light buff.
30 × 25 × 14 mm. Account of threshed barley.

1) 60+20+1+[x š]e gur-sag-gál-si-sá
2) UD-bi
3) še-giš-ra-a

4) sig₇ a-šà ^{d}En-líl-lá

Rev. 5) ugula Sag-du₅

(space)

6) ⌈mu⌉ 5+[4]?

116. (AO 11355)

Acquisition Genouillac, June 22, 1929. Light buff.
26 × 22 × 13 mm. Account of goats, sheepskins, and
goatskins.

1) 1 máš zag-nu-šuš

2) 1 máš zag-šuš

3) Ur-^{d}Šara-ka

4) 1 máš zag-nu-šuš

Lo.E. 5) 1 kuš u₈ zag-šuš

Rev. 6) 1 kuš ùz zag-šuš

7) Ur-^{d}EN.ZU

8) Ezen-^{d}Dumu-zi-da

U.E. 9) ^{d}Utu-mu

L.E. 10) 8 mu 1 iti

117. (AO 11356)

Acquisition Genouillac, June 22, 1929. Light gray.
28 × 25 × 13 mm. Account of threshed barley.

1) 13? še gur-sag-gál

2) En₅-si-gal

3) še-giš-⌈ra-a⌉

4) ⌈sig₇ BAR.DU⌉

Rev.   (destroyed, no signs visible

now. The Louvre catalogue

reads: "An 6, 7^e mois.")

118. (AO 11357)

Acquisition Genouillac, June 22, 1929. Light buff. 24 × 22 × 12 mm. Account of one goatskin.

1) 1 kuš ùz
2) udu ur$_4$-ra
3) Bar-bi
4) A-⌈bí?-nar⌉?-e

Rev. 5) mu-DU
6) 3 mu 8 iti

119. (AO 11358)

Acquisition Genouillac, June 22, 1929. Light buff. 29 × 23 × 14 mm. Account of sheep and goats.

1) 1 udu-nita
2) Ur-^{d}Šara
3) 1 máš-nita
4) Ur-^{d}EN.ZU
5) Lugal-e?-gi-e?

Rev. 6) ba?-DU?
    (space)
7) 21+[x mu x i]ti

120. (AO 11359)

Acquisition Genouillac, June 22, 1929. Light gray. 30 × 26 × 13 mm. Account of threshed barley.

1) 360 lá 11 še gur-sag-gál-si-sá
2) Ur-^{d}Ki-nà(d)
3) še-giš-ra-a
4) sig$_7$ a-šà ^{d}En-líl-lá

Rev. 5) Lugal-KA-e

6) šu-ba-ti

(space)

7) 4 iti

121. (AO 11360)

Acquisition Genouillac, June 22, 1929. Light gray.
32 × 25 × 14 mm. Account of threshed barley.

1) 105 še gur-sag-gál-dùl

2) Lugal-KA

3) še-giš-ra-a

4) sig$_7$ a-šà gibil

Rev. 5) ⌈uru?-a⌉ (𒌷𒆲𒁀) ba-si

(space)

6) [x mu x]+4 iti

122. (AO 11361)

Acquisition Genouillac, June 22, 1929. Light buff.
27 × 23 × 13 mm. Account of one goatskin.

1) 1 kuš ùz-ama zag-šuš

2) Ur-^{d}Šara-kam

3) A-bí-nar-e

4) mu-DU

Rev. 5) Umma^{KI}

(space)

6) 4 mu

123. (AO 11362)

Acquisition Genouillac, June 22, 1929. Light buff.
36 × 28 × 15 mm. Account of one goatskin and of one
sheep.

            1)   1 kuš ⌈udu⌉-nita zag-šuš
            2)   1 sila₄-nita ša-dug
            3)   Lugal-KA-kam
            4)   ⌈d⌉Utu-mu sipa
            5)   6 mu 3 iti
    Rev.   (uninscribed)

                124. (AO 11363)

Acquisition Genouillac, June 22, 1929. Light buff.
36 × 28 × 14 mm. Witnessed memo concerning the deposition of silver with a person. Plate XIX.
            1)   1 lá igi-4-gál kug gín
                    (wr. ....KUG.GÁL.GÍN)
            2)   Ur-é AB Tu-tu-da
            3)   Lugal-KA-e
            4)   ì-da-tuku
            5)   ▨ -gi simug
    Rev. 6) Ur-zu ašgab
            7)   lú-ki-inim-ma-me
            8)   4 mu 12 iti

                125. (AO 11364)

Acquisition Genouillac, June 22, 1929. Buff. 29 ×
26 × 13 mm. Receipt of barley.
            1)   190 še gur-sag-gál-si-sá
            2)   Ra-bal-e (clear)
            3)   šu-ba-ti
            4)   [še] zi-ga
            5)   Lugal-K⌈A⌉
    Rev.   (space)

6) 5 mu 6? iti

126. (AO 11365)

Acquisition Genouillac, June 22, 1929. Light buff.
28 × 23 × 13 mm. Account of three sheepskins?

      1) 3 k[uš? u_8]?

      2) Na-EŠ-dù-a

      3) [E]n-za-bar

      4) Zag-mu [x](𒀸)-da-[nothing?]

Rev. 5) mu-laḫ₄(DU.DU)-ḫi-éš

        (space)

      6) 25 mu

127. (AO 11366)

Acquisition Genouillac, June 22, 1929. Light buff.
25 × 24 × 12 mm. Account of one sheepskin.

      1) 1 kuš udu-nita

      2) zag-šuš

      3) Ur-^{d}Šara

      4) ^{d}Dumu-zi-an-dùl

Rev. 5) [mu-DU]

        (space)

      6) 4 mu

128. (AO 11367)

Acquisition Genouillac, June 22, 1929. Light buff.
27 × 26 × 13 mm. Account of sheepskins.

      1) [x] kuš u[du]?

      2) Ama-é

      3) [x] kuš u_8

4)   [PN]?

Rev. 5)   [ki A?-s]ar-[til]?-a-ta

6)   mu- ⟨signs⟩ -éš

7)   23?+[x]? mu [x] i[ti]

129. (AO 11368)

Acquisition Genouillac, June 22, 1929. Dark gray.
In two small fragments. Nothing recognizable.

130. (AO 11369)

Acquisition Genouillac, June 22, 1929. Light buff.
28 × 25 × 13 mm. Some forms of numbers are pointed;
cf. AO 11402. Signs without meaning. Probably a
school exercise.

1)   ⟨sign⟩   ma-na

2)   ⟨sign⟩   lá ⟨sign⟩   gál

3)   ⟨signs⟩
     (unfinished)

Rev.   (uninscribed)

131. (AO 11370)

Acquisition Genouillac, June 22, 1929. Gray. 32 ×
28 × 14 mm. Pointed forms of numbers. Account of
onions.

1)   420+30 sum-bal sa

2)   240+30 sum sa

3)   é-a ì-gál
     (rest destroyed)

132. (AO 11371)

Acquisition Genouillac, June 22, 1929. Light buff
to gray. 55 × 40 × 17 mm. Context unrecognizable.
Its meaning depends on lú-šu in line 10. Or read lú
šu ba-DU-me and link šu with DU(=túm?)?

1) 1 Ur-^{d}šara
2) 1 Da-d⌈a⌉
3) Ur-⌈ša$_6$-ga⌉ nu-banda ba-DU.DU
4) 1 Ur-ku-ma
5) ŠUBUR dub-⌈sar⌉ ba-DU
6) 1 Ur-ur
7) Da-da dumu-sipa-dè ba-DU
8) 1 UŠ.KU
9) I-ku-ku dam-gàr ba-DU
Rev. 10) lú-šu ba-DU-me
11) É-úr ugula-bi

133. (AO 11372)

Acquisition Genouillac, June 22, 1929. Light buff.
35 × 30 × 13 mm. Pointed forms of numbers. Account
of goats and sheep.

1) 5 máš
2) 2 udu-nita
3) Ur-^{d}šara-ka-kam
4) 3 u$_8$-ama
5) Lugal-KA-⌈kam⌉
Rev. 6) bar zú(KA)-si-
7) ka-ta
8) ^{d}Utu-mu-gi$_4$
9) sipa-dè

-77-

10) ba-DU.DU

11) 4 mu 8 iti

134. (AO 11373)

Acquisition Genouillac, June 22, 1929. Gray. 49 ×
37 × 16 mm. Account of copper objects.

1) 5 urudu-šum

2) É-kug

3) dam Ur-^{d}ŠÈ.NIR

4) 2 Kur-ra

5) 1 Ur-du$_6$

6) urudu-šum á(ID)

7) šu-ba-ti

8) urudu-šum zi-ga

Rev. 9) Ama-é

10) dam Ur-^{d}Šara-ka

(space)

11) 3 mu

135. (AO 11374)

Acquisition Genouillac, June 22, 1929. Light buff.
43 × 30 × 15 mm. Account of sheep.

1) 26 udu-u$_8$-ama

2) 26 udu-nita

3) 7 SAL-sila$_4$ šà-dùg

4) 6 sila$_4$-nita šà-dùg

5) udu Lugal-KA-kam

Rev. 6) É-gud-da

7) ì-da-sig$_7$

(no date)

136. (AO 11375)

Acquisition Genouillac, June 22, 1929. Light buff
to gray. 33 × 28 × 14 mm. Account of threshed
barley, emmer, and wheat.

        1) 186(gur) 2(pi) še gur-sag-gál
               (wr. GÁL.ŠE.GUR.SAG)
        2) 10(gur) 1á 2(pi) zíz gur
        3) 4(gur) 2(pi) gig <gur>
        4) [še]-giš-ra-⌈a⌉
Rev. 5) ^dŠara-an-dùl
        6) a-šà
        7) ŠIR.BUR.LA^{KI}
           (space)
        8) 4 mu 5 iti

137. (AO 11376)

Acquisition Genouillac, June 22, 1929. Light buff.
37 × 33 × 16 mm. Account of five goats.

        1) 5 máš šà-dùg
        2) GIŠ.MI š⌈u-i⌉?
        3) a-šà Àm-ma-
        4) ta mu-^{DU}_{DU}
        5) Ur-sipa-da udu
        6) A-bí-nar
Rev. 7) máš zi-ga

138. (AO 11377)

Acquisition Genouillac, June 22, 1929. Light buff.
42 × 28 × 17 mm. Pointed forms of numbers. Account
of sheep and goats.

-79-

1) 1? udu-nita

2) Ur-^{d}Šara

3) [udu]? Ur-^{d}EN.ZU

4) ba-tag

5) 2 máš-nita

6) 1 ùz

7) pisan-udu-ka

Rev. 8) ^{d}Utu-mu-gi$_4$-e

9) bí-gi$_4$

10) udu zi-ga

11) Lugal-e

12) 22 mu 10 lá 1 iti

139. (AO 11378)

Acquisition Genouillac, June 22, 1929. Light buff.
45 × 32 × 13 mm. Account of goatskins.

1) 2 kuš ùz zag-šuš

2) 1 kuš ùz zag-nu-šuš

3) Ur-^{d}Šara-ka-kam

4) 3 kuš ùz zag-šuš

5) 1 kuš ùz zag-nu-šuš

6) Ur-^{d}EN.ZU-kam

7) en$_5$-si ŠUKU.^{d}INNIN-ka

Rev. 8) mu ti-la-a

9) ^{d}Dumu-zi-an-dùl-e

10) mu-DU

(space)

11) 3 mu 10 iti

140. (AO 11379)

Acquisition Genouillac, June 22, 1929. Gray. 44 ×
34 × 19 mm. Account of barley.

1) 360+12(gur) 2(pi) <še> gur-sag-gál

2) a-šà i-ku$_6$(ḪA)

3) $^{<d>}$Geštin-an-ka

4) 120+21 še gur-sag-gál

5) A.É(=É.A = é-dur$_5$?) Lugal-šà-ga

Rev. (uninscribed)

141. (AO 11380)

Acquisition Genouillac, June 22, 1929. Light buff.
40 × 32 × 15 mm. Account of one goatskin.

1) 1(𒁹) kuš máš zag-šuš

2) Ur-^{dx}Šara-ka-kam

3) ^{d}Utu-mu-gi$_4$ sipa

(space)

4) 4 mu 10 iti

Rev. (uninscribed)

142. (AO 11381)

Acquisition Genouillac, June 22, 1929. Light gray.
37 × 31 × 15 mm. Pointed forms of numbers. 60 gur
is written horizontally; units for 1-9 gur are
written vertically (slightly slanted). Account of
threshed barley and emmer. Plate XX.

1) 90 lá 1 še gur-sag-gál-dùl

2) 25(gur) ziz Da-da

3) 91(gur) 𒐕 še gur

4) Ur-zu(wr. SU)

-81-

        5) ugula Lugal-nagar-zi

        6) 20 zíz gur

        7) Šeš-tur

Rev. 8) še-giš-ra-a Y (of no importance)

        9) sig$_7$ Sug-gal

             (space)

        10) 5 iti

143. (AO 11382)

Acquisition Genouillac, June 22, 1929. Light buff.
40 × 32 × 15 mm. Account of wheat and emmer.

        1) 10 gig gur-sag-gál

        2) 20 zíz gur

        3) Du-du nu-banda É-sikil

        4) 5 zíz gur

        5) Dug$_4$-ga nu-banda

Rev. 6) 10(gur) Ur-^{d}Lum-ma sanga

             (no date)

144. (AO 11383)

Acquisition Genouillac, June 22, 1929. Gray to
black. 35 × 28 × 16 mm. Account of threshed barley.

        1) 66 še gur-sag-gál

        2) É-e

        3) 120 lá 5 še gur

        4) KA-ma-DINGIR

        5) še-giš-ra-a

Rev. 6) sig$_7$ a-šà ^{d}En-líl-lá

        7) ugula Ur-^{d}Ab-ú

             (space)

8) 4 iti

145. (AO 11384)

Acquisition Genouillac, June 22, 1929. Light buff.
42 × 33 × 15 mm. Account of threshed barley.

1) 127+[x še gur]-sag-gál-d[ùl]
2) Ur-íd
3) še-giš-ra-a
4) sig₇ BAR.DU
5) Lú-pàd-da
6) šu-ba-ti
7) A-pi₄-sal₄^{⟨KI⟩}

Rev.   (space)

8) 5 mu 4 i[ti]

146. (AO 11385)

Acquisition Genouillac, June 22, 1929. Light buff.
63 × 41 × 19 mm. Account of sheep and goats.

1) lá-ni 135 udu-nita
2) 22 u₈-ama
3) 31 ùz-ama
4) 13 máš-nita
    (double line)
5) šu-nigín 201 udu-ḫi-a
6) lá-ni En-an-ni sipa-da
7) ì-da-sig₇
8) 50 lá 1 (pointed forms of
        numbers) síg lá-ni ma-na

Rev. 9) En-an-ni sipa-da ì-da-gál
        (no date?)

147. (AO 11386)

Acquisition Genouillac, June 22, 1929. Light buff-gray. 44 × 33 × 17 mm. Pointed forms of numbers. Account of goats.

1) 3 úz-ama
2) 1 máš
3) su₇( )-e ba-kú
4) 1 máš
5) Lu-lu
6) máš zi-ga
Lo.E. 7) ᵈ⌈Utu⌉-mu sipa
(space)
8) 7 mu 8 iti

148. (AO 11387)

Acquisition Genouillac, June 22, 1929. Light buff-gray. 54 × 37 × 18 mm. Pointed forms of numbers. Account of sheep and goats.

1) 12 u₈-ama
2) 6 udu-nita
3) 14 úz-ama
4) 6 SAL.ÁŠ.GÀR šà-dùg
5) Ki-KU-lú sipa-da
6) ì-da-sig₇
7) Lugal-KA-e
8) ì-šid
Rev. 9) gaba-ru É-gal baḫarₓ
(wr. U.EDIN)-ka
10) a-[š]à gibil
(space)
11) 11 mu 1 iti

-84-

149.   (AO 11388)

Acquisition Genouillac, June 22, 1929.   Light buff.
67 × 42 × 17 mm.   Account of fields.

1) 3(bur) a-ša gán

2) A.SAG.UL.DU

3) 4(bur) a-šà ^{d}Dumu-zi-da

4) 2(bur) a-šà A-suḫur?()-ra

5) 4(bur) ŠA-gal

6) 3(bur) Lugal-ra-mu-gi$_{4}$

7) 2(bur) da ki-gur$_{7}$-ka
   (double line)

8) šu-nigín 20 lá 2(bur) a-šà
   gán

9) Ama-é dam

Rev. 10) Ur-^{dš}ara-ka

150.   (AO 11389)

Acquisition Genouillac, June 22, 1929.   Buff-gray
to black.   60 × 46 × 20 mm.   Witnessed contract concerning the purchase of a person.   Plate XXI.

1) 8 kug gín

2) níg-ŠÁM+A Ur-LI GAR

3) Ur-LI Si$_{4}$-si$_{4}$ ama-[ni]

4) Lugal-iti-da šu-ne-ne [ab-si]

5) giš-gan-na ab-ta-b[al]

6) ì sag-gá-šè sag-gá-[b]i

7) a ba-sum Inim-ma-ni

8) lú-níg-ŠÁM+A-ag-à[m]

9) Si$_{4}$-si$_{4}$ lú-níg-ŠÁM+A-kú-[àm]

Rev. 10) 1 Ka-k[ug]

-85-

11) dumu Lugal-níg-zu

12) 1 ^{d}En-líl-lá-mu-gi$_4$

13) dumu Íl [nothing]?

14) 1 LUGAL-pum dub-sar

15) 1 Lugal-giš

16) Pi-li-li (sic)

17) Ur-^{d}ŠE.TIR (sic)

18) dumu Ur-^{d}En-ki-ka

19) 1 Zag-⌜mu⌝ dumu A-zu-zu

20) 1 Lugal-ka-⌜gi-na⌝ dam-gàr

L.E. 21) lú-ki-inim-ma-bi-me

151. (AO 11390)

Acquisition Genouillac, June 22, 1929. Buff to gray.
66 × 44 × 20 mm. Witnessed contract concerning the
purchase of a field. Plate XX.

1) 2(iku) gán da E+PAB dub-sar-ka

2) an-gál

3) níg-šám-bi

4) 4 kug gín

5) ud še kug-ga 2(pi) gur
   al-šá(m)(⟨⟩)-gá

6) 3 še gur

7) 20(silà) zíd-ba 10(silà) ì-silà

8) Ne-sag nin(SAL.TÚG) Nu-nu-ke$_4$

9) šu-ba-ti

10) ud gán-ga lú ù-ma-a dù-a
    (all clear)

Rev. 11) 2(iku) gán-bi-še

12) 4(iku) gán ab-ši-gá-gá

-86-

13) Inim-ma an-gál

14) 1 Lugal-lá Ur-dun

15) lú-inim-ma-bi

16) Lú-na-nam simug

17) lú-šám-ag-àm

18) Ne-sag nin(SAL.TÚG) Nu-nu

19) lú-šám-kú-àm

152. (AO 11391)

Acquisition Genouillac, June 22, 1929. Buff. 68 ×
58 × 21 mm. Witnessed contract concerning the purchase of a field. Plate XXII.

i 1) 6+2(iku) gán

2) E+PAB dub-sar-ka

3) níg-šám-pi

4) 1/2 kug ma-na 2 gín

5) 2 še gur

6) 1 bar-túg

7) 2(pi)(⌑) še-ba

8) É-ki-dùg-ga

9) Da-pi-$_{DU}^{DU}$

10) Ur-PA

11) dumu-ni šu-ba-ti

ii 1) gán-⌐pi⌐ ⌐lugal⌐ mu-[x]

2) .[...](⌐)

3) mu-[x]

4) 1 A-ba-[^{d}En-líl? dumu]?

5) Lugal-[....]

6) 1 Ḫar-A[N-.... dumu]?

7) Amar-[....]

         8) lú-[ki-inim]-ma-[pi-me]

         9) L[ugal-....]

        10) [....]

        11) [....]

Rev. i   (beginning destroyed)

          (rest uninscribed)

            153. (AO 11392)

Acquisition Genouillac, June 22, 1929. Reddish buff.
59 × 60 × 22 mm. Witnessed contract concerning the
purchase of a field. Plate XXIII.

    i 1) 6(iku) gán é-ad(⌐∏⊏)

      2) níg-šám-bi

      3) 10 lá 1 kug gín

      4) 7 še gur

      5) 1 bar-túg 2 še gur-kam

      6) Lú-ḫé-gál

      7) dumu Igi-mi-mi-ke$_4$

      8) šu-ba-ti

      9) 2(∏) kug gín

   ii 1) A-ba-^{d}En-líl

      2) dumu Šà-dingir-zu-ke$_4$

      3) ba-DU šám ⊞ -AN

      4) ud ^{lú}-ma dù-da-a
          $_{dingir}$

      5) Dingir-gá-ab-e

      6) arád Igi-mi-mi-ke$_4$

      7) dam dumu-ni

      8) igi-ba-a DU-a

      9) Inim-ma-ni GAR

     10) Lugal-KA-šè

                    -88-

Rev. i 1) SIMUG
     2) lú-šám-ag-AN⌄
     3) ᵈUtu-IM.MI^mušen
         (wr. UD.ḪU.MI.AN.IM)
     4) dumu Ba-za
     5) Temen-an-ni
     6) dumu Amar-ki
  ii 1) lú-ki-inim-ma-[bi]-me
         (rest destroyed)
         (probably nothing missing)

(AO 11393 = Ur III administrative text).

154. (AO 11394)

Acquisition Genouillac, June 22, 1929. Gray. 66 ×
37 × 18 mm. Pointed forms of numbers. Account of
fields.

     1) 1(bur) gán
     2) Lugal-⌈TUR⌉.ŠÈ
     3) 1(bur) Nigìn
     4) 6(iku) Sag-ḫul-a
     5) 6(iku) Lú-ᵈŠara
     6) 1(bur) Ka-kug
     7) 1(bur) ᵈEn-líl-da
     8) 6(iku) UŠ.KU
     9) 6(iku) Lugal-gar
    10) [x(iku) I]nim-zi-da
    11) [x(iku) Da]?-ša₆
    12) [x(iku) Lu]gal-KA
  Rev. 13) [x(iku)] Ur-igi

14) [x(iku) X]-ni

15) [6+6](iku) Ur-LI

16) ⌈1⌉(bur) Sag-a-du

17) 6+6(iku) UŠ.KU ŠU.ḪA

18) 6(iku) Su-BAPPIR.A

19) 6(iku) Da-da

20) 6+6(iku) ^{d}Dumu-zi-da

21) 6(iku) PAB

22) 6(iku) Ur-^{d}Nin-tu

155. (AO 11395)

Acquisition Genouillac, June 22, 1929. Gray. 52 × 39 × 19 mm. Witnessed contract concerning the purchase of a field. Plate XXIV.

1) 1 1/2(iku) gán

2) gán da é Tu-tu-ka-kam

3) níg-ŠÁM+A-bi

4) 2 1/2 kug gín

5) Lugal-níg-zu

6) šu-ba-ti

7) Inim-ma-ni

8) í-na-lá

9) Lugal-níg-zu

Rev. 10) lú-níg-ŠÁM+A-kú-<àm>

11) Inim-ma-ni

12) lú-níg-ŠÁM+A-ag-àm

(double line)

13) 1 ⌈Da⌉-ša$_6$

14) dumu Me-lám-⌈an⌉-ni

15) 1 Lugal-e[n]-nu

16) dumu Ama-zu-zu

17) 1 A-⌈du⌉-nà(d) nagar

18) 1 Lugal-iti-da

19) Pi-li-li (sic)

L.E. 20) lú-ki-inim-ma-bi-me

156. (AO 11396)

Acquisition Genouillac, June 22, 1929. Light buff.
52 × 36 × 16 mm. Account of sheep and goats. Plate
XXI.

1) 10 udu-nita zag-šuš

2) 2 ùz zag-šuš

3) 6 máš-nita zag-šuš

4) 5(𒐅) máš šà-dùg zag-nu-šuš-àm

5) udu zi-ga-àm

6) É-lú sipa

7) 7 máš-gal-gal

8) máš É-gal-kam

9) máš sag-ba ba-an-íl-šè

Rev.   (space)

10) Ur-^{d}Šara-ke$_4$

11) máš zi-da

12) ì-tur$_x$(𒋲) DU-a

13) Ad-da SILÀ.ŠU.DU$_8$

14) du$_6$-AB-ta

15) mu-DU.DU

16) 20 lá 1 mu 10 iti

157. (AO 11397)

Acquisition Genouillac, June 22, 1929. Light buff to
gray. 45 × 32 × 15 mm. List of five persons.

1) 1 [PN]
2) 1 Ma-ni
3) 1 LUL.A
4) 1 Me-a
5) 1 ERIN-da-ni
   (double line)
6) dumu Nigìn-me
7) [....] (perhaps nothing)

Rev.   (uninscribed)

158. (AO 11398)

Acquisition Genouillac, June 22, 1929. Buff to black.
Top destroyed. 44 × 47 × 18 mm. Witnessed contract
concerning the purchase of a person? Plate XXII.

(beginning destroyed)
1') šu-ne-ne ab-si
2') Inim-ma-ni-e
3') ì-ne-lá
4') Ka-kug ama-ni
5') Lugal-túg-maḫ ugula-ni
6') lú-níg-ŠÁM+A-kú-àm-me?!
7') Inim-ma-ni-e

Rev. 8') lú-níg-ŠÁM+A-ag-àm
9') mu lugal-šè
10') mu Nam-maḫ-[šè] (space for one
        very short sign, such as [šè])
11') K[A-bi a]l-til
12') [la-ba-gi₄-gi₄]-da
13') [....-m]u?
        (rest destroyed)
L.E. 1') lú-ki-[inim-ma-bi-me]
-92-

159. (AO 11399)

Acquisition Genouillac, June 22, 1929. Light buff.
45 × 32 × 15 mm. Account of goatskins and goats.

        1) 1 [kuš ....]

        2) Ur-[....]

        3) Ur-^{d}.[...](✳)-ke$_4$

        4) ba-DU

        5) 1 kuš máš zag-šuš Ur-^{dx}Šara

             (PN added in small signs)

        6) Lugal-kur sipa-e mu-DU

        7) 1 máš zag-nu-šuš

Rev. 8) A-bí-ra

        9) Ur-^{d}EN.ZU-ka-kam

     10) Lugal-kur sipa

            (space)

     11) 8 [mu ....]

160. (AO 11400)

Acquisition Genouillac, June 22, 1929. Violet/red
tinge on brown background. 55 × 43 × 20 mm. List
of names of workers?

        1) Ur-nigín

        2) Bu-zu-zu

        3) Šu-Ma-ma

        4) PÙ.ŠA-an-ni

        5) DINGIR-iš-da-gal

        6) Da-gi-zi

   Rev. 7)

        8) SIKIL?.NE?

(AO 11401 = Ur III administrative text)

-93-

161. (AO 11402)

Acquisition Genouillac, June 22, 1929. Buff to gray.
47 × 38 × 17 mm. Some forms of numbers are round,
others pointed; cf. AO 11369. While all signs are
clear, the meaning of the text is not understandable.

    1) OOD 𒌑 lú

    2) A. ⧫ -me

    3) DD DD 𒌋 EME.GIR$_x$(ŠÈ)

    (end)

Rev.   (uninscribed)

162. (AO 11403)

Acquisition Genouillac, June 22, 1929. Light buff.
36 × 27 × 14 mm. Account of linen garments.

    1) 3 gada-bar-si

    2) Lugal-níg-UL(⧫)

    3) 3 Ur-dam

    4) 3 Ur-ša$_6$-ga

    5) 2 Ur-sag

    6) 7 É-zi

    7) 3 Ur$_4$-šà

Rev.   (space)

    8) šu-nigín 20 gada-bar-si

    9) A-ga-dè^{KI}

    10) ba-DU

    (space)

    11) 4 mu 11 iti

163. (AO 11404)

Acquisition Genouillac, June 22, 1929. Buff-gray.
42 × 34 × 16 mm. Pointed forms of numbers. 60 is
written horizontally. Cf. also AO 11405 and 11409.
Size of a field, with lines 1-4 giving its four sides,
and line 5 its area. The figures do not fit. Plate
XXIII.

    1) 115 gar-du uš sig(⧖)-ta
    2) 70 gar uš igi-nim
    3) 66 gar sag igi-nim
    4) 56 gar <sag> sig(⧖)-ta
        (space)
Rev. 5) ⧄ ⪤ (iku) gán

164. (AO 11405)

Acquisition Genouillac, June 22, 1929. Buff-gray.
47 × 36 × 17 mm. Text very badly preserved; apparently similar to AO 11404 and 11409.

    1) 60+50 ⚹ ? <gar>? sig?-ta?
    2) 60+20+5 gar 2 kuš-numun
        igi-nim-ma
    3) 540(9 × 60) lá 50 uš
    4) 30+⌈x⌉ sag
Rev.   (8 horizontal lines)

165. (AO 11406)

Acquisition Genouillac, June 22, 1929. Buff-gray.
38 × 35 × 17 mm. Pointed forms of numbers. Account
of garments.

    1) 20 túg níg-⌈lám⌉ [?]

    2) 11 ⌈túg⌉ ŠÁ.GI.URUDU
    3) 20 lá 3? túg šà-ga-dù
    4) 7 túg A.SU
Rev.   (uninscribed)

(AO 11407 = Ur III administrative text)
(AO 11408 = Ur III administrative text)

166. (AO 11409)

Acquisition Genouillac, June 22, 1929. Light buff
to gray. 52 × 40 × 16 mm. Pointed forms of numbers.
60 is written horizontally. Cf. also AO 11404 and
11405. Size of a field, with lines 1-4 giving its
four sides, and line 5 its area. The figures fit
approximately. Plate XXIII.

    1) 63 𐎗 gar-du uš <igi-nim>
    2) 22 𐎗 <gar-du> sag íd-da
    3) 90 <gar-du> uš sig(𐎗)-ta
    4) 22 𐎗 <gar-du> sag a-gar-ra
    5) 𐎗𐎗 (iku) gán giš-ùr-ra
    6) LUL.A ašgab
Rev.   (uninscribed)

167. (AO 11410)

Acquisition Genouillac, June 22, 1929. Light buff.
68 × 40 × 17 mm. Pointed forms of numbers. The
meaning of numbers found after some personal names
is not clear. Lines 2, 3, 5, 7, and 14 are clearly
indented. Account of workers.

1) 30 lá 1 guruš 24
2)   A[d?-x]
3)   É?-e
4) 20 lá 3 Lú-^dŠara 16
5)   Lugal-še
6) 15 UŠ.KU šu-i(𒌋) 13
7)   Lugal-nagar-zi
8) 23 Ab-kid 20
9) 22 UŠ.KU É-li 25
10) Ur-^dAb-ú
    (double line)
11) 20+[x] Ur-lú 15
Rev. 12) gud ^d[....]
13) 15 [....]
14)   Lug[al-....]
15) 22+[x₂...]
16) Ur-^{GIŠ}gigir .[...]
17) 13+[2] ⌈Ú⌉?-na-ap-[....]
    (double line)
18) 14 Ur-éš-1[íl]
19) Ur-PA

168. (AO 11411)

Acquisition Genouillac, June 22, 1929. Gray. 72 ×
42 × 20 mm. Contents not understandable. Plate XXIV.

1) ŠUBUR dub-sar
2) Tir-kug-gi
3) Si-kug-é
4) Du-bi UŠ.KU
5) UŠ.KU Ba-al(𒍤𒀀)-ni

6) Lugal-e sipa

7) En-an-na-DU

8) Lugal-zag-gi-si

9) en$_5$-si ⌈SU.KUR.RU^{KI}⌉ ( )

10) GAL.ZU-⌈d⌉?[....]

11) ME-^{d}[....]

    (rest destroyed)

Rev.   (beginning destroyed)

1') [A]mar-lú ugula

    (end)

169. (AO 11412)

Acquisition Genouillac, June 22, 1929. Gray to black. 94 × 46 × 25 mm. Witnessed contract concerning the purchase of two fields. Plate XXV.

1) 6(iku) gán da ki-ša-nu-dar()-
    ra-ni

2) níg-ŠÁM+A-bi 10 kug gín

3) Lugal-al-e

4) šu-ba-ti

5) 6(iku) gán da ki-ša-nu-dar()-
    ra-ni

6) níg-ŠÁM+A-bi 10 kug gín

7) Ab-zu

8) Igi-zi-bi

9) šu-ba-ti-[é]š

10) Inim-ma-ni

11) ì-na-[lá]

12) Lugal-a[l]

13) Ab-⌈zu⌉

-98-

14) Igi-zi

15) dumu Ne-sag ašgab-me

16) lú-níg-ŠÂM+A-kú-a-me

Rev. 17) Inim-ma-ni

18) lú-níg-Š[ÂM+A-ag]-[à]m

19) [1 X](🔲)-lul-lul X(🔲)

20) 1 Lugal-giš

21) dumu Ne-sag ugula

22) 1 Ka-kug

23) dumu Lugal-níg-zu

24) 1 Ur-nigìn(UD.É) dumu-ni

25) 1 Da-ša₆

26) dumu Me-lám-an-ni

27) 1 Ur-ša₆-[ga]

28) [dumu] É?-a?

29) 1 ᵈEn-líl-li-dingir-[zu]

30) dumu Ka-kug [nothing?]

31) 1 É-EZEN-rí-e engar?

(double line)

32) lú-ki-inim-ma-bi-[me]

170. (AO 11413)

Acquisition Genouillac, June 22, 1929. Light buff.
Perforated cone, 60 mm. high and diameter of 40 mm.
Now published by M. Lambert in AOr XXXV (1967) pp.
521ff. Witnessed memo concerning an oath? taken by
one person. Plate XXV.

1) [m]u lugal-šè(🔲)

2) [m]u sanga IN(🔲)ᴷᴵ-šè(🔲)

3) ⌈É⌉-úr dumu Lugal-uru-na-[ke₄]?

-99-

4) [L]ú-na-nam dumu Lugal-K[A]?
   simug-da
5) [g]iš?(𒄑) ì-da-TAR
6) lú-lú la-ba-g[i₄-da]
7) Ne-sag ašgab
8) Ka-kug-ga-ni dumu Kur-rí-◁[...]
9) Ur-si₄-si₄ dumu Nin-gá
10) lú-ki-inim-ma-pi-me

INDICES OF PROPER NAMES

1. Personal Names

    The personal names are arranged in the order of
the Latin alphabet. The logograms occurring in the
Akkadian names have not been transliterated into
Akkadian but retained in their Sumerian form in har-
mony with the transliterations in the main part of
this volume.

    The following abbreviations for genealogical
relationships are used in this list: s. for son,
d. for daughter, gs. for grandson, f. for father,
m. for mother, gf. for grandfather, br. for brother,
sis. for sister, h. for husband, and w. for wife.
The entry (f.n.) stands for a feminine personal name.

A-[....o], 11307:8

A-a-bí-nar, 11337:2; 11345:2

   A-a-<bí>-nar, 11328:2

A-ba: DINGIR-ba-ni šu A-ba, 8638:11

A-ba-an-da-di s. of Kum-ku-šè, 11309:14

A-ba-^{d}En-líl, 11130:18

   A-ba-[^{d}En-líl? s.]? of Lugal-[....], 11391 ii 4

   A-ba-^{d}En-líl s. of Šà-dingir-zu, 11392 ii 1

A-bí-GI$_4$, 11328:7

A-bí-nar, 11268:9; 11341:3; 11346:2; 11361:3,
     11376:6

   A-⌈bí?-nar⌉?, 11357:4

   A-bí-nar sipa, 11267:18; 11292:19; 11298:7;
     11315 rev. i 2; 11335:3

Ama-UM+ME.GA, 11264:2;   11290:12
Ama-zu-zu f. of Lugal-e[n]?-nu, 11395:16
Amar-[....] f. of Ḫar-A[N-....], 11391 ii 7
Amar-ki f. of Temen-an-ni, 11392 rev. i 6
[A]mar-lú ugula, 11411:1'
Ar-na-ba, 8642:2

Ba-al-ni UŠ.KU, 11411:5
Ba-bi, 11278:10
Ba-za, 11313:6
   Ba-za f. of ᵈUtu-IM.MI^mušen, 11392 rev. i 4
Bala-ki, 11274:15
Bar-bi, 11346:4;   11357:3
Bar-ra-ni-še s. of MES-kisal-li, 11309:10
Barag-ga-ni lú-tir, 11273:5
Barag-nita, 11255:3, 7, 11, 16
Barag-si-ga, 11258:9
Be-lí-GÀR, 8640:2
Be-lí-lí, 8640:4
Bu-zu-zu, 11400:2

Da-áš-lul, 11286:2
Da-bu-a, 11312:14
Da-da, 11263:5;   11271:11;   11381:2;   11394:19
   Da-da?, 11265:13
   [D]a?-da, 11311:3
   Da-d[a], 11371:2
   Da-da dumu-kar, 11273:4
   Da-da dumu-sipa, 11371:7
   Da-da f. of UŠ.KU, 11313:8
-103-

Da-gi-zi, 11400:6

Da-pi-DU.DU f. of Ur-PA, 11391:9

Da-⌈ša₆⌉, 11303:15

   Da-[ša₆], 11308:15

   Da⌉?-ša₆, 11394:11

   ⌈Da⌉-ša₆ s. of Me-lám-⌈an⌉-ni, 11395:13

   Da-ša₆ s. of Me-lám-an-ni, 11412:25

   Da-ša₆ br. of Ne-sag, s. of Me-lám-an-ni, 11320:11

Dam-da-[li]k (f.n.), 8961:2

Dan-ì-lí, 8959:11

DINGIR, see after Ì-lí-

Du-bi UŠ.KU, 11411:4

Du-du, 11313:4

   Du-du KI.BE, 11273:6

   Du-du nu-banda É-sikil, 11382:3

   Du-du f. of Ur-mes, 11304:5

Du₆-ba-al, 11274:12

Dug₄-ga nu-banda, 11382:5

ᵈDumu-zi-an-dùl, 11318:6; 11322:5; 11378:9;
      11366:4; 11352:5

ᵈDumu-zi-da, 11394:20

E-lam, 11254 rev. i 7

É?-a f. of Ur-ša₆-[ga], 11412:28

É-a-ba-lik NAR, 8638:12

É-a-ra-bí, 8641:4

É-da-lu: dam É-da-lu MU(-ke₄), 11310:19

É-e, 11264:8; 11305:2; 11383:2

   É?-e, 11410:3

   É-e ugula, 11305:7

É-EZEN-rí-e, 11317:18

    É-EZEN-rí-e engar?, 11412:31

É-gal, 8637:3; 11396:8

    É-gal baḫar, 11343:7

    É-gal baḫar$_x$, 11387:9

É-gud, 11285:3; 11374:6

    É-gud(wr. GUD+⸢), 11257:13

É-kalam f. of Sag-^{d}En-líl-da, 11317:3

É-ki-dùg-ga, 11391:8

É-kug w. of Ur-^{d}ŠE.NIR, 11373:2

É-li, 11410:9

É-lú sipa, 11396:6

⸢É⸣-maḫ-da f. of Sá-lim-mu, 11130:8

É-úr ad-kub$_x$, 11312:12

    É-úr ugula, 11371:11

    ⸢É⸣-úr s. of Lugal-uru-na, 11413:3

É-zi, 11403:6

    É-zi lú Ur-zu, 11130:16

En-an-na-DU, 11411:7

    En-an-na-DU en$_5$-si Umma^{KI}, 11307:13

En-an-ni, 11257:12; 11265:7; 11269:4; 11271:8;
        11314:14, 16

    En-an-ni sipa, 11385:6, 9

^{d}En-líl-.[...], 11319:15

^{d}En-líl-da, 11394:7

^{d}En-líl-dingir-zu s. of Ka-kug, 11319:5; see ^{d}En-líl-li

    ^{d}En-líl-li-dingir-⸢zu⸣ s. of Ka-kug, 11412:29

^{d}En-líl-[lá] nu-[S]AR?, 11131:24

^{d}En-líl-lá-mu-gi$_4$ s. of Íl, 11389:12

^{d}En-líl-li, 11309:5; see ^{d}En-líl-dingir-zu

^dEn-líl-li s. of Ka-kug ugula udul, 11316:21

En-na-na s. of DINGIR-⌈a⌉-zu, 8638:8

En-šagana sag-apin gud ^{dš}Šara, 11325:2

En-za-bar, 11323:4

   [E]n-za-bar, 11365:3

En₅-si-gal, 11356:2

ERIN-da-ni br. of Ma-ni, LUL.A, and Me-a, s. of
       Nigìn, 11397:5

GAL.ZU-⌈d⌉?[....], 11411:10

Gemé-è-a, 11269:10; 11271:10, 13

GIŠ.MI, 11274:12

   GIŠ.MI š⌈u⌉-⌈i⌉?, 11376:2

   GIŠ.MI(-na), 11275:13

GUR₈-gu-LUM, 11273:1; 11350:7

Ḫa-lum (or X-ḫa-LUM), 8636:7

ḪAL-ì-⌈lum⌉, 10330:3

Ḫar-A[N-.... s.]? of Amar-[....], 11391 ii 6

I-da-da, 8637:4

I-da-DINGIR, 8960:2, 7, 12, 25

I-gu-núm DAM.GÀR, 8638:4

I-ku-ku dam-gàr, 11371:9

[I]-nin-la-ba s. of SIG₅-DINGIR, 8959:14

I-ti-^dDa-gan, 11254 rev. i 6

Ì-li w. of DINGIR-an-dùl, 11307:5

Ì-lí-iš-da-gal, 8959:3

   [Ì]-lí-iš-da-gal, 8961:4

Ì-lí-sa-lik, 7983:3

DINGIR-⌈a⌉-zu f. of En-na-na, 8638:9

DINGIR-an-dùl h. of Ì-li, 11307:6

DINGIR-ba-ni, 11130:19

   DINGIR-ba-ni šu A-ba, 8638:10

DINGIR-ga-lí, 11340:4

DINGIR-gá-ab-e arád Igi-mi-mi, 11392 ii 5

DINGIR-iš-da-gal, 11400:5

DINGIR-ma-LÚ, 11286:8

DINGIR-su-a-ḫa s. of ⌈Na⌉-ni, 8960:20

Íd-ḫi-nun nu-gig, 11259:10

IGI.DU GAL₀NI, 11317:10

Igi-mi-mi f. of Lú-ḫé-gál, 11392:7, ii 6

Igi-⌈nin⌉, 11285:5

Igi-zi br. of Ab-zu, s. of Ne-sag ašgab, 11412:8, 14

Íl f. of ^{d}En-líl-lá-mu-gi₄, 11389:13

Im-ta, 11254 rev. i 3

Im$_x$(DU)-da-lik, 8959:17

Inim-ma, 11130:5?, 13; 11390:13

Inim-ma-ni, 11316:7, 13; 11317:7; 11320:7; 11389:7;
       11392 ii 9; 11395:7, 11; 11398:2', 7';
       11412:10, 17

   Inim-ma-ni maškim, 11309:17

Inim-ma-ni-zi-da, 11332:4; 11338:2

Inim-zi baḫar$_x$, 11274:14

Inim-zi-da, 11260:8

   [I]nim-zi-da, 11394:10

Ka-kug, 11273:3; 11394:6; 11398:4' (here f.n.!)

   Ka-kug ugula uru, 11309:13

   Ka-k[ug] s. of Lugal-níg-zu, 11389:10

Ka-kug s. of Lugal-níg-zu f. of Ur-nigìn, 11412:22

Ka-kug ugula udul f. of ^{d}En-líl-li, 11316:22

Ka-kug f. of ^{d}En-líl-dingir-zu, 11319:6

Ka-kug f. of ^{d}En-líl-li-dingir-[zu], 11412:30

Ka-kug f. of Ur-^{d}Dumu-zi-da and Lú-ti-dingir-zu,
11320:16

Ka-kug-ga-ni s. of Kur-rí-.[...], 11413:8

KA-ma-DINGIR, 11383:4

^{d}KA-Me-ir, 8960:24

KA-šè, 11263:4; 11273:7

Ki-KU-lú sipa, 11387:5

Ki-sar, 11317:2

Kud-du, 11307:2

Kum-ku-šè f. of A-ba-an-da-di, 11309:15

Kur-ra, 11373:4

Kur-rí-.[...] f. of Ka-kug-ga-ni, 11413:8

Li-li f. of Lugal-giš, 11317:12

Lu-lu, 11318:9; 11386:5

Lú-[x-x], 11131:23

Lú-^{d}Aš-šir-gi$_{4}$, 11254 ii 2

Lú-^{d}Ba-ú, 11293:3

Lú-barag-[g]i f. of [L]ú-giš, 11310:14

Lú-giš, 11310:7, 13

   [L]ú-giš s. of Lú-barag-[g]i, 11310:14

Lú-ḫé-gál s. of Igi-mi-mi, 11392:6

Lú-na-nam simug, 11390:16

   [L]ú-na-nam simug, 11310:15

   [L]ú-na-nam s. of Lugal-K[A]? simug, 11413:4

Lú-nigir, 11275:7

Lú-pàd-da, 11384:5

Lú-^{d}Šara, 11394:5; 11410:4

Lú-ti-dingir-zu br. Ur-^{d}Dumu-zi-da, s. of Ka-kug,
    11320:15

Lugal-⌈....⌉, 11270:3'

  L⌈ugal-....⌉, 11391 ii 9

  Lug⌈al-....⌉, 11410:14

  Lugal-[....] f. of A-ba-[^{d}En-líl]?, 11391 ii 5

Lugal-ab, 11263:3

  [Lugal]-ab, 11313:2

  Lugal-ab BALA.KI, 11274:15

Lugal-al, 11412:3, 12

Lugal-an-ni, 11260:6

  Lugal-an-[ni]? s. of Ur-^{d}EN.ZU, 11307:9

Lugal-AŠ-ni, 11270:8, 11278:7

Lugal-barag, 11278:5

Lugal-DU, 11273:9

Lugal-e, 11377:11

  [Lu]gal-e, 11312:15

  Lugal-e sipa, 11411:6

Lugal-e-gi, 11332:2; 11338:3; 11350:6

  Lugal-e?-gi, 11358:5

Lugal-e[n]?-nu s. of Ama-zu-zu, 11395:15

Lugal-engar-dùg dam-⌈gàr⌉, 11317:13

Lugal-gar, 11394:9

Lugal-giš, 11389:15

  Lugal-giš s. of Li-li, 11317:11

  Lugal-giš s. of Ne-sag ugula, 11412:20

Lugal-iti-da, 11389:4; 11395:18

Lugal-KA, 11262:7; 11263:10; 11274:2; 11279:18;

                    11290:3;   11293:4;   11296:2;   11301:2;
                    11306:13;   11339:4;   11341:4;   11342:5;
                    11343:4;   11347:5;   11359:5;   11360:2;
                    11362:3;   11363:3;   11372:5;   11374:5;
                    11387:7

   Lugal-K[A], 11281:4'

   Lugal-K⌈A⌉, 11364:5

   [Lu]gal-KA, 11394:12

   Lugal-KA ugula, 11301:7, 8

   Lugal-K[A]? simug f. of [L]ú-na-nam, 11413:4

Lugal-ka-⌈gi-na⌉ dam-gàr, 11389:20

Lugal-KA-gu-la, 11307:11

Lugal-KA-šè simug, 11310:18;   11392 ii 10

Lugal-kalag-zi f. of ME-an-ni, 11131:14

Lugal-kar-e-si lú-má-gur$_8$ f. of UŠ.KU, 11290:2

Lugal-kur sipa, 11399:6, 10

Lugal-lá, 11390:14

Lugal-nagar-zi, 11287:12;   11296:12;   11410:7

   Lugal-nagar-zi ugula, 11381:5

Lugal-níg, 11264:4

Lugal-níg-ba É/DAG.DÙG dam-gàr, 11290:11

Lugal-níg-UL, 11403:2

   Lugal-níg-UL h. of Ama-na-nam, 11275:11

Lugal-níg-zu, 11395:5, 9

   Lugal-níg-zu f. Ka-k[ug], 11389:11

   Lugal-níg-zu f. of Ka-kug gf. of Ur-nigìn,
   11412:23

LUGAL-pum dub-sar, 11389:14

Lugal-ra-mu-gi$_4$, 11388:6

Lugal-SAG, 11288:4;   11311:9

Lugal-⌈sár?-ra⌉?, 11310:8

Lugal-si, 11263:7

Lugal-šà, 11319:13

   Lugal-ša₆ s. of Ur-PA, 11309:8

Lugal-šà-ga, 11379:5; see also A.É Lugal-šà-ga
        under Locations

Lugal-še, 11305:9; 11410:5

   Lugal-še [u]gula, 11305:14

Lugal-šu-maḫ sipa, 11299:3

Lugal-tar, 11343:3

Lugal-tir, 11284:8

Lugal-túg-maḫ, 11317:9

   Lugal-túg-maḫ ugula, 11398:5'

Lugal-TUR.ŠÈ, 11296:4; 11301:3

   Lugal-⌈TUR⌉.ŠÈ, 11394:2

Lugal-uku-⌈gá⌉ s. of ⌈U⌉r-éš-⌈líl⌉, 11317:16

Lugal-uru-na f. of ⌈É⌉-úr, 11413:3

Lugal-zag-gi-si en₅-si ⌈SU.KUR.RU^{KI}⌉, 11411:8

LUL.A ašgab, 11409:6

  LUL.A, br. of Ma-ni, Me-a, and ERIN-da-ni, s. of
     Nigìn, 11397:3

Lul-gu-ag, 11270:6

Ma-ni, 11397:2

ME-^{d}[....], 11411:11

ME-an-ni s. of Lugal-kalag-zi, 11131:13

⌈ME-^{d}IM⌉, 11263:1

ME-nigìn, 11312:5

ME-šeš-šeš dub-sar, 11131:25

Me-a br. of Ma-ni, LUL.A, and ERIN-da-ni, s. of

Nigin, 11397:4

Me-lám-[an]-ni f. of ⌈Da⌉-ša₆, 11395:14

  Me-lám-an-ni f. of Da-ša₆, 11412:26

  Me-lám-an-ni f. of Ne-sag and Da-ša₆, 11320:13

Me-me (f.n.), 7983:4

Me-zu dub-sar, 11259:5

MES-kisal-li f. of Bar-ra-ni-še, 11309:11

Mes-ZU.AB, 11319:12

Mi-su₄-a s. of ⌈Ur⌉-mes, 8960:26

Mu-ni, 11282:8

Mušen-dù, 11263:2

Na-na, 11286:6

⌈Na⌉-ni f. of DINGIR-su-a-ḫa, 8960:20, 21

⌈Na-ra-am⌉-ᵈEN.ZU, 11130:6, 11

Nam-maḫ, 11398:10'

Nam-ti-la, 11269:6, 8

Nam-ti-la-ni, 11271:4, 14

Ne-sag, 11296:15

  Ne-sag ašgab, 11413:7

  Ne-sag ašgab, f. of Ab-zu and Igi-zi, 11412:15

  Ne-sag br. of Da-ša₆, s. of Me-lám-an-ni, 11320:12

  Ne-sag ugula f. of Lugal-giš, 11412:2

  Ne-sag sis. of Nu-nu, 11390:8, 18

NI-za-za, 8642:3

Níg-du₈-du₈, 11286:5

Nigin, 11285:9; 11296:6; 11301:4; 11394:3

  Nigin f. of Ma-ni, LUL.A, Me-a, and ERIN-da-ni, 11397:5

Nin-dug₄-ga, 11131:22

Nin-gá f. of Ur-si₄-si₄, 11413:9

Nin-maš s. (or d.) of Nin-pàd-da, 11316:3, 4

Nin-mes, 11284:2

Nin-níg-x w. of ⌈A⌉-zu-[zu], m. of Zag-mu, 11320:5, 8

Nin-níg-zu, 11274:5

Nin-pàd-da m. of Nin-maš, 11316:5, 11

Nin-ra, 11130:9, 12

Nin-ú f. of Ur-ki, 11274:3

Nir-d[a?-....], 11281:3'

Nu-ni-tum, 8638:6

Nu-nu sis./br. of Ne-sag, 11390:8, 18

PAB, 11394:21

Pi-li-li, 11389:16; 11395:19

Pù-DINGIR, 8637:5; 8641:2

Pù-sa-GI ENGAR, 8639:5

PÙ.ŠA-an-ni, 11400:4

Ra-bal, 11364:2

    Ra-bal ugula 11342:7

Sá-lim-mu s. of ⌈É⌉-maḫ-da, 11130:8

Sag-a-du, 11394:16

Sag-du₅, 11287:7

    Sag-du₅ ugula, 11278:18; 11354:5

    Sag-du₅ f. of UŠ, 11131:4, 15

Sag-ᵈEn-líl-da s. of É-kalam, 11317:4

Sag-ḫul-a, 11394:4

Sar-ga-lí-LUGAL-ri LUGAL A-ga-dèᴷᴵ, 11131:10

Si-dù, 11296:10

    Si-dù sipa, 11262:9; 11300:6

Si-ku-sum, 8642:4

Si-kug-é, 11411:3

Si$_4$-si$_4$ m. of Ur-LI, 11389:3, 9

SIG$_5$-DINGIR f. of [I]-nin-la-ba, 8959:15

SILA.ŠU.DU$_8$-maḫ f. of UŠ, 11131:5, 12

Su-BAPPIR.A, 11394:18

Šà-da dub-sar, 11280:11

Šà-dingir-zu f. of A-ba-^{d}En-líl, 11392 ii 2

Šà-ga-ni dub-sar, 11274:16

^{d}Sara-an-dùl, 11375:5

Šeš-a, 11286:9, 12

^{d}ŠEŠ-sipa, 11275:1

Šeš-tur, 11274:11; 11381:7

^{d}ŠEŠ.KI-e-zu-a, 11275:2

Šu-Ma-ma, 11400:3

Šu-me, 11312:18

ŠUBUR dub-sar, 11371:5; 11411:1

Temen-an-ni s. of Amar-ki, 11392 rev. i 5

Tir?-kug sipa f. of Ú⌈r?-ni? a⌉šgab?, 11316:20

Tir-kug-gi, 11411:2

Tu-tu, 11363:2; 11395:2

Ú-ba-ru AB+ÁŠ.URU^{KI}, 8643:2

Ú-da, 11259:7

⌈Ú⌉?-na-ap-[....], 11410:17

UD-bi, 11354:2

Um-mi-mi, 11286:7

UN-íl dím, 11299:2

Ur-[....], 11399:2

Ur-^d.[...], 11399:3

Ur-A.LÙ.ZA, 11342:2; see also A.LÙ.ZA under Locations

Ur-ab, 11288:2; 11311:7

Ur-^dAb-ú, 11287:4; 11410:10

   Ur-^dAb-ú ugula, 11383:7

Ur-d⌈a⌉?, 11311:11

Ur-^dDa-mu uku-uš ugula-é, 11319:8

Ur-dam, 11260:4; 11287:10; 11403:3

   [U]r-dam, 11324:2

   Ur-dam ugula, 11288:7

Ur-du-du, 11259:6

   Ur-du-du s. of Ur-PA, 11130:14

Ur-du$_6$, 11263:12; 11286:4; 11373:5

Ur-^dDumu-zi-da br. of Lú-ti-dingir-zu, s. of Ka-kug,

      11320:14

Ur-dun, 11390:14

Ur-é, 11363:2

   Ur-é ugula-é, 11273:8

Ur-^dEn-dím-gi[g]?, 11259:2

Ur-^dEn-ki f. of Ur-^{dx}ŠE.TIR, 11389:18

Ur-^dEn-líl-lá, 11260:2

Ur-^dEN.ZU, 11261:15; 11262:11; 11266:12; 11267:17;

      11272:12; 11273:12; 11277:10; 11281:2';

      11283:17; 11297:7; 11300:7; 11302:4;

      11315 ii 8; 11322:4; 11326:3; 11327:4, 6;

      11333:5; 11335:2; 11339:6; 11341:2;

      11350:5; 11355:7; 11358:4; 11377:3;

      11378:6; 11399:9

[U]r-^{d}EN.ZU, 11279:15

U[r-^{d}EN.ZU], 11292:15

Ur-^{d}EN.ZU f. of Lugal-an-[ni]?, 11307:10

Ur-éš-l[íl], 11410:18

⌈U⌉r-éš-⌈líl⌉ f. of Lugal-uku-⌈gá⌉, 11317:17

Ur-^{giš}gigir, 11263:8; 11410:16

⌈Ur⌉-^{giš}gigir, 11305:13

Ur-gu, 11259:6

Ur-gu nu-banda, 11310:9

Ur-íd, 11384:2

Ur-igi, 11329:3; 11394:13

Ur-^{d}IM, 11319:11

Ur-^{d}Innin, 11319:4

Ur-kalag-ga lú-erín, 11130:21

Ur-ki s. of Nin-ú, 11274:3

Ur-^{d}Ki-nà(d), 11347:2; 11359:2

Ur-ku-ma, 11371:4

Ur-kud, 11270:2; 11278:3; 11349:2

Ur-kun sipa, 11274:8

Ur-LI, 11394:15

⌈Ur⌉-LI, 11285:13

Ur-LI s. of Si$_4$-si$_4$, 11389:2, 3

Ur-lú, 11410:11

Ur-lú lú-ŠIM+GAR, 11273:10

Ur-^{d}Lum-ma sanga, 11382:6

Ur-mes, 11263:11; 11319:14

[Ur-mes] sukal, 11289:1'

Ur-mes zadim, 11312:17

Ur-mes s. of Du-du, 11304:4

[Ur]-mes f. of Mi-su$_4$-a, 8960:5

Ur-^{d}Nagar UŠ.KU, 11259:4

Ur-^{d}Nin-NAGAR.GÍD, 11284:12

   Ur-^{d}Nin-NAGAR.GÍD sipa, 11312:11

   Ur-^{d}Nin-NAGAR.GÍD udul, 11277:11

   Ur-^{d}[Nin-NAGAR.GÍD] ud[ul], 11281:6'

Ur-nigìn, 11400:1

   Ur-nigìn(UD.É) s. of Ka-kug gs. of Lugal-níg-zu,
      11412:24

Ur-^{d}Nin-tu, 11394:22

Ur-PA, 11130:19; 11410:19

   Ur-PA dub-sar, 11313:10

   Ur-PA s. of Da-pi-DU.DU, 11391:10

   Ur-PA f₀ of Lugal-ša$_6$, 11309:9

   Ur-PA f. of Ur-du-du, 11130:15

Ur-sag, 11403:5

Ur-sag-pa-è (a-šà), 11345:3

Ur-si$_4$-si$_4$ s. of Nin-gá, 11413:9

Ur-sipa sipa, 11268:11

   Ur-sipa-da, 11376:5

   Ur-sipa-da sipa na-ga-da, 11267:20

   Ur-sipa-da sipa na-gada, 11315 rev. i 4

Ur-ša$_6$, 11296:8; 11351:3

Ur-ša$_6$-ga, 11282:4; 11403:4

   Ur-ša$_6$-[ga], 11317:15

   Ur-⌈ša$_6$-ga⌉ nu-banda, 11371:3

   Ur-ša$_6$-g[a] SILÀ.ŠU.DU$_8$, 11259:3

   Ur-ša$_6$-[ga] [s. of] É?-a, 11412:27

   Ur-ša$_6$-⌈ga⌉ lú Ur-^{d}Šara, 11320:9

Ur-^{d}Šara, 11257:11; 11258:6; 11261:9; 11262:5;
      11267:8; 11272:8; 11277:6; 11279:8;

                11281:8;   11283:9;   11291:4;   11292:8;

                11297:4;   11298:6;   11300:3;   11314:13;

                11315:8;   11318:7;   11321:4;   11322:2;

                11326:5;   11332:6;   11333:3;   11334:2;

                11337:6;   11338:5;   11339:2;   11350:3;

                11353:7;   11355:3;   11358:2;   11361:2;

                11366:3;   11371:1;   11372:3;   11377:2;

                11378:3;   11380:2;   11396:10;   11399:5

Ur-^{d}Šara dub-sar, 11300:4

Ur-^{d}Šara dub-sar dingir-ra, 11262:12

Ur-^{d}Šara h. of Ama-é, 11304:3;   11373:10;

        11388:10

Ur-^{d}Šara: Ur-ša$_{6}$-⌈ga⌉ lú Ur-^{d}Šara, 11320:10

Ur-^{d}[ŠE.T]IR? KA.SAR.RA, 11259:14

Ur-^{d}ŠE.TIR s. of Ur-^{d}En-ki, 11389:17

Ur-^{d}ŠÈ.NIR h. of É-kug, 11373:3

Ur-šubur GIŠ.TÚG.KAR.DU, 11259:10

Ur-temen lú-ŠIM+GAR, 11274:13

Ur-^{d}TUR, 11263:6, 9;   11305:6

Ur-ur, 11282:11;   11371:6

⌈Ur⌉-^{d}Utu, 11285:11

Ur-^{d}Utu sipa, 11318:3

Ur-zu, 11254 rev. i 4;   11331:2;   11340:2;

        11348:2

    Ur-zu (wr. SU), 11381:4

    Ur-zu ašgab, 11363:6

    Ur-zu? dí[m]?, 11259:14

    Ur-zu f. of ⌈A⌉-bu-ḫa-DU, 11290:10

    Ur-zu: É-zi lú Ur-zu, 11130:17

Ur-ZU∘AB GAL.NI, 11309:12

                        -118-

Úr-kug-gi, 11312:4

Ú⌈r?-ni? a⌉šgab? s. of Tir?-kug sipa, 11316:19

Ur₄-šà, 11403:7

UŠ s. of Sag-du₅, 11131:4, 15

  UŠ s. of SILÀ.ŠU.DU₈-maḫ, 11131:5, 12

UŠ-da-da, 11130:2, 10

UŠ.KU, 11264:2; 11311:5; 11317:19; 11371:8;
      11394:8; 11410:9

  UŠ.KU dub-sar, 11343:6

  UŠ.KU sipa, 11296:17

  UŠ.KU ŠU.ḪA, 11394:17

  UŠ.KU šu-i, 11260:11; 11311:14; 11330:4;
     11410:6

  UŠ.⌈KU⌉ šu-i, 11324:5

  UŠ.KU s. of Da-da, 11313:8

  UŠ.KU s. of Lugal-kar-e-si lú-má-gur₈, 11290:2

UŠ.KU-tur, 11327:3

Uš-su-da, 11353:2

ᵈUtu-gar, 11274:10

ᵈUtu-ḫi-li, 11285:7

ᵈUtu-IM.MI^mušen s. of Ba-za, 11392 rev. i 3

ᵈUtu-mu, 11258:7; 11272:17; 11283:19; 11355:9

  ᵈUtu-mu sipa, 11261:17; 11262:13; 11291:6, 7;
     11297:9; 11300:12; 11318:13; 11322:7;
     11333:7; 11339:7; 11348:3; 11362:4

  ᵈ⌈Utu⌉-mu sipa, 11386:7

ᵈUtu-mu-gi₄, 11377:8

  ᵈUtu-mu-gi₄ sipa, 11321:5; 11331:3; 11334:3;
     11372:8; 11380:3

Wa-dar-i-li NAR, 8638:14

Zag-mu, 11130:18; 11309:6 (perhaps not a PN);
          11317:14; 11365:4

   Zag-⌈mu⌉ s. of A-zu-zu, 11389:19

   Zag-mu [s.] of ⌈A⌉-zu-[zu] and Nin-níg-x, 11320:2, 4

Zu-zu, 11254 rev. i 5

^d[....], 11410:12

^d[...] s. of [....], 11316:15

[....] f. of ^d[...], 11316:16

⌈d?_{X-x-iš}⌉?-da-[gal], 11274:9

⌈X⌉-du, 11312:16

⌈X⌉-gi simug, 11363:5

⌈X⌉-ḫa-LUM (or Ḫa-lum), 8636:7

[X]-lul-lul, 11412:19

⌈X⌉-ma, 11295:12

[X]-ni, 11394:14

[X-š]eš, 11270:10

2. Divine Names

^dAb-ú, see PN Ur-^dAb-ú

^dAš-šir-gi₄, see PN Lú-^dAš-šir-gi₄

^dBa-ú, see PN Lú-^dBa-ú

^dDa-gan, see PN I-ti-^dDa-gan

^dDa-mu, see PN Ur-^dDa-mu

^dDumu, see ^dTUR

^dDumu-zi, see PNs ^dDumu-zi-an-dùl, ^dDumu-zi-da,
          Ur-^dDumu-zi-da; see also a-šà ^dDumu-zi-da
          under Locations; see also Ezen-^dDumu-zi-da
          under Temporal Terms

^d[D]UN, see PN Ur-^d[D]UN?

É-a, see PN É-a-ba-lik

^dEn-dím-gi[g]?, see PN Ur-^dEn-dím-gi[g]?

^dEn-ki, see PN Ur-^dEn-ki

^dEn-líl, see PNs A-ba-^dEn-líl, ^dEn-líl-[...],
        ^dEn-líl-da, ^dEn-líl-dingir-zu, ^dEn-líl-[lá],
        ^dEn-líl-lá-mu-gi₄, ^dEn-líl-li, ^dEn-líl-li-
        dingir-⌈zu⌉, Ur-^dEn-líl-lá; see also a-šà
        ^dEn-líl-lá under Locations

^dEN.ZU, see PNs ⌈Na-ra-am⌉-^dEN.ZU, Ur-^dEN.ZU

^{<d>}Geštin-an-ka, see a-šà i-ku₆ ^{<d>}Geštin-an-ka
        under Locations

^dIM, see PNs ⌈ME-^dIM⌉, Ur-^dIM

I-nin, see PN [I]-nin-la-ba

^dInnin, 11352:3; 11378:7; see PN Ur-^dInnin; see
        also a-šà ^dInnin under Locations

KA, see PNs KA-ma-DINGIR, Lugal-KA

   ^dKA, see PN ^dKA-Me-ir

   Pù, see PN Pù-DINGIR

   Pum, see PN LUGAL-pum

^dKi-nà(d), see PN Ur-^dKi-nà(d)

^dLum-ma, see PN Ur-^dLum-ma

Ma-ma, see PN Šu-Ma-ma

^dNagar, see PN Ur-^dNagar

^dNin-NAGAR.GÍD, see PN Ur-^dNin-NAGAR.GÍD

^dNin-tu, see PN Ur-^dNin-tu; see also a-šà ^dNin-tu
        under Locations

^dNisaba, 11269:7

Pù, see KA

Pum, see KA

^{d}Šara, 11325:3; see also PNs Lú-^{d}Šara, ^{d}Šara-an-dùl,
    Ur-^{d}Šara

^{d}ŠE.TIR, see PN Ur-^{d}ŠE.TIR

^{d}ŠÈ.NIR, see PN Ur-^{d}ŠÈ.NIR

^{d}ŠEŠ, see PN ^{d}ŠEŠ-sipa

^{d}ŠEŠ.KI, see PN ^{d}ŠEŠ.KI-e-zu-a

^{d}Tišpak, see PN A-bî-^{d}Tišpak

^{d}TUR, see PN Ur-^{d}TUR

^{d}Utu, see PNs Ur-^{d}Utu, ^{d}Utu-gar, ^{d}Utu-ḫi-li,
    ^{d}Utu-IM.MI^{mušen}, ^{d}Utu-mu, ^{d}Utu-mu-gi$_4$

3. Geographic Names

A-ga-dè^{KI}, 8636:6; 11131:11; 11254 i 3; 11403:9

A-pi$_4$-sal$_4$$^{<KI>}$, 11384:7

AB.INNIN^{KI}, 11255:12

IN^{KI}, 11130:22; 11413:2;

Na-EŠ-dù-a, 11262:14; 11283:20; 11300:13
    Na-EŠ-dù-a^{KI}, 11323:3

⌈SU.KUR.RU^{KI}⌉, 11411:9

ŠIR.BUR.LA^{KI}, 11375:7

Tu-tu^{KI}, 8640:5

Umma^{KI}, 11307:14; 11361:5

4. Locations

A.É (=É.A?) Lugal-šà-ga, 11379:5; see also PN
    Lugal-šà-ga

A.LÙ.ZA: TÚG.ŠUM A.LÙ.ZA, 11284:7, 11
    sig$_7$ A.LÙ.ZA, 11301:6; 11306:4

ŠE.KIN.T[AR]? A.LÙ.ZA-ka, 11314:19

A-sar-AN.TI.LA-(šè), 11353:5

   [A?-s]ar-[til]?-a-(ta), 11367:5

a-šà, see also under sig₇ a-šà

a-šà A-suḫur?-ra, 11388:4

a-šà Àm-ma-ta, 11376:3

a-šà ^{d}Dumu-zi-da, 11388:3

a-šà ì-ku₆ $^{<d>}$Geštin-an-ka, 11379:2

a-šà ŠIR.BUR.LA^{KI}, 11375:7

a-šà Ur-sag-pa-è-ta, 11345:3

a-ùr-ra, 11271:2

AN.KI.KI-(šè), 11335:4

BÀD LUGAL, 11254 i 8

da GIŠ.ḪAR?, 11269:3

du₆-AB-ta, 11396:14

du₆-NISABA(inversum)^{SAR}, 11305:17

e nar-ka-am, 11271:6

É.A-maš-zu, 11328:3

É.A-si₄-na, 11267:16; 11283:18; 11294:6;
        11315 rev. i 1

é-DUB ⌈gu⌉-la-a, 11344:2

é-DUB ⌈tur⌉-a, 11344:5

é du₆-k⌈a⌉, 11269:5

É LUGAL, 11254 ii 6

é nam-zu ÉŠ.KA, 11269:7

é-sikil (nu-banda), 11382:3

é zag-mu-ta, 11309:6 (or Zag-mu = PN)

(gán) a-gar-ra, 11409:4

gán A.SAG.UL.DU, 11388:2

gán da é Tu-tu-ka-kam, 11395:2

(gán) da ki-gur$_7$-ka, 11388:7

gán da Ki-ša-nu-dar-ra-ni, 11412:1, 5

gán E+PAB dub-sar-ka, 11390:1; 11391:2

gán é-ad, 11392 i 1

gán giš-ùr-ra, 11409:5

gán-maḫ?, 11269:9

(gán) ŠA-gal, 11388:5

GIŠ.AŠ ^{d}Nisaba, 11269:7

íd-da, 11409:2

igi-nim, 11404:2, 3

   igi-nim-ma, 11405:2

ME.NI (udu), 11261:16

nag-kud Inim-ma-ni-zi-da-šè, 11332:4

   nag-kud Inim-ma-ni-zi-da-ka, 11338:2

pisan-udu-ta, 11271:3; 11337:3

   pisan-udu-ka, 11377:7

sig-ta, 11404:1, 4; 11405:1?; 11409:3

sig$_7$ a-šà ^{d}En-líl-lá, 11278:15; 11296:13; 11306:8;
       11342:4; 11349:3; 11351:5; 11354:4;
       11359:4; 11383:6

sig$_7$ a-šà gán-gíd-a, 11336:5

sig$_7$ a-šà gibil, 11288:6; 11305:16; 11360:4;
       11387:10 (wr. a-[š]à gibil)

sig$_7$ a-šà ^{d}Innin, 11296:18

sig$_7$ a-šà ^{d}Nin-tu, 11306:6

sig$_7$ Amar-ú-ga, 11329:4

sig$_7$ BAR.DU, 11260:10; 11282:12; 11287:17;
       11296:20 (wr. BAR.DU); 11311:13; 11313:11;
       11324:4; 11330:3; 11347:4; 11356:4;
       11384:4

sig$_7$ Sug-gal, 11381:9

su$_7$ Uš-su-da, 11353:2

ŠUKU.^{d}INNIN-ka (en$_5$-si), 11352:3; 11378:7

tir Ur-^{d}EN.ZU-ka-kam, 11273:12

URU^{KI} (in AB+ÁŠ.URU^{KI}), 8643:3

    uru-a, 11271:6

    uru-si[g$_4$-?], 11269:2

^{d}ZA.GÀR-dug$_4$-ga-ka (skin), 11327:2

5.   Temporal Terms

Ezen-^{d}Dumu-zi-da, 11355:8

    Ezen-^{d}Dumu-zi-ka (wr. Ezen-DUMU.AN.ZI.KA),

        11321:6

Ezen-MURUB$_4$-ka, 11335:5

^{ITI}Ha-ni-it, 8959:19

CATALOGUE OF TABLETS

Acquisition Ihler, between 1921 and 1922 (No. 1)

1. AO 7983   Dark gray. 26×24×10 mm. Receipt of
              barley. Plate I.

Acquisition Géjou, 1923, from Tell Asmar? (Nos. 2-9)

2. AO 8636   Brown-gray. 60×44×17 mm. Account of
              silver, an equid, oxen, and barley.
              Plate I.

3. AO 8637   Brown. 49×41×17 mm. Account of
              barley. Plate I.

4. AO 8638   Dark gray. 46×31×15 mm. Witnessed
              contract concerning the purchase of
              gold. Plate I.

5. AO 8639   Dark gray. 34×32×14 mm. Receipt of
              sheep, goats, and silver. Plate II.

6. AO 8640   Brown. 36×30×14 mm. Account of
              barley. Plate II.

7. AO 8641   Brown. 36×30×14 mm. Issue of
              barley. Plate II.

8. AO 8642   Light brown. 32×30×16 mm. Account
              of goatskins. Plate II.

9. AO 8643   Dark gray. 22×22×11 mm. Receipt of
              barley. Plate III.

Acquisition 1924 (Nos. 10-12)

10. AO 8959   Reddish-brown. 68×41×18 mm. Account
    of barley. Plate IV.

11. AO 8960   Brown. 92×40×30 mm. Account of
    barley. Plate IV.

12. AO 8961   Dark gray. 28×26×12 mm. Receipt of
    an unknown commodity.

Acquisition Géjou, December 1925 (No. 13)

13. AO 10330 Brown. 75×52×24 mm. Account of a
    beer ingredient called BAPPIR and
    of flour.

Acquisition David, December 22, 1927 (Nos. 14-15)

14. AO 11130 Gray. 63×35×17 mm. Witnessed con-
    tract concerning a field. Note oath
    by Narâm-Sin. Plate V.

15. AO 11131 Dark gray. 74×42×18 mm. Witnessed
    contract concerning the purchase of
    ten gur of dates. Note oath by
    Šar-kali-šarrī. Plate III.

Acquisition Genouillac, June 22, 1929 (Nos. 16-170)

16. AO 11254 Dark gray. 86×74×21 mm. Two-column
    tablet. Issue of barley. Plate VI.

17. AO 11255 Light buff. 57×35×16 mm. Account
    of wool. Plate V.

18. AO 11256   Light buff. 70×44×19 mm. Almost
                completely effaced. Text treats of
                animals.

19. AO 11257   Light buff-gray. 58×46×19 mm.
                Account of sheep and goats. Plate
                VII.

20. AO 11258   Light buff-gray. 56×33×16. Account
                of goats.

21. AO 11259   Light buff. 69×45×19 mm. Issue of
                barley.

22. AO 11260   Light buff. 65×36×18 mm. Account
                of threshed barley.

23. AO 11261   Light brown. 69×45×18 mm. Account
                of sheep and goats.

24. AO 11262   Light buff. 63×41×17 mm. Account of
                goatskins, goats, and sheep. Plate
                VII.

25. AO 11263   Light gray. 56×35×18 mm. Pointed
                forms of numbers. Account of barley?
                of nine different persons in three
                groups.

26. AO 11264   Light gray. 56×38×16 mm. Pointed
                forms of numbers. Account of barley.

27. AO 11265   Light buff. 57×34×20 mm. Reverse
                badly effaced. Witnessed contract
                concerning sheep, goats, and wool.
                Plate VIII.

28. AO 11266   Light buff. 62×39×18 mm. Pointed
              forms of numbers in front of (mu).
              Account of cattle, sheep, and goats.

29. AO 11267   Light buff. 80×48×21 mm. Account
              of sheep and goats.

30. AO 11268   Light buff-gray. 71×41×18 mm.
              Reverse effaced. Account of goats
              and sheep.

31. AO 11269   Light buff. 68×42×19 mm. Reverse
              effaced. Text similar to AO 11271.
              Account of gifts of sheep and goats.
              Plate IX.

32. AO 11270   Brown-gray. 62×42×20 mm. Pointed
              forms of numbers. Account of barley.
              Plate IX.

33. AO 11271   Light buff. 63×42×18 mm. Text is
              similar to AO 11269. Account of
              gifts of sheep and goats. Plate VIII.

34. AO 11272   Light buff. 65×42×18 mm. Account of
              sheep and goats.

35. AO 11273   Light buff. 62×39×19 mm. Account
              of barley.

36. AO 11274   Buff-gray. 57×38×18 mm. Witnessed
              loan of silver. Plate IX.

37. AO 11275   Light buff. 58×35×18 mm. Memo
              concerning the dwelling right of a
              person and about his? commodities

deposited with two persons. Plate X.

38. AO 11277   Light buff. 60×39×18 mm. Pointed
                 forms of numbers in front of (mu).
                 Text similar to AO 11281. Account
                 of cattle.

39. AO 11278   Buff. 62×37×17 mm. Account of
                 threshed barley and emmer. Plate X.

40. AO 11279   Light buff. 64×44×18 mm. Account
                 of sheep and goats. Plate XI.

41. AO 11280   Light buff. 73×32×16 mm. Memo
                 concerning various commodities de-
                 posited by one person. Plate X.

42. AO 11281   Light buff. 72×45×17 mm. Pointed
                 forms of numbers in front of (mu).
                 Text similar to AO 11277. Account
                 of cattle.

43. AO 11282   Dark gray, almost black. 46×31×16
                 mm. Issue of barley.

44. AO 11283   Light buff. 68×40×18 mm. Account
                 of sheep and goats. Plate XII.

45. AO 11284   Gray-buff. 66×46×20 mm. Account
                 of barley.

46. AO 11285   Light buff. 44×34×18 mm. Covered
                 with salts; needs cleaning. Account
                 of sheep and goats.

47. AO 11286   Light buff. 38×30×15 mm. Issue of
                 flour. Plate XI.

48. AO 11287   Dark gray. 76×42×18 mm. Account of
                threshed barley, emmer and wheat.

49. AO 11288   Light gray. 35×29×14 mm. Account
                of threshed barley.

50. AO 11289   Light buff. 47×37×16 mm. Memo con-
                cerning various commodities deposited
                with one person. Plate XII.

51. AO 11290   Gray. 46×33×18 mm. Witnessed con-
                tract concerning the purchase of an
                equid. Plate XIII.

52. AO 11291   Light buff. 40×31×16 mm. Account
                of goats and sheep.

53. AO 11292   Light buff. 65×44×17 mm. Account
                of goats and sheep.

54. AO 11293   Gray. 36×27×15 mm. Memo concerning
                barley and emmer.

55. AO 11294   Gray. 43×36×17 mm. Account of
                sheep.

56. AO 11295   Light buff. 66×52×22 mm. Account
                of goats and sheep. Plate XIII.

57. AO 11296   Gray. 66×37×17 mm. Account of
                threshed barley and emmer.

58. AO 11297   Light buff. 66×38×17 mm. Account
                of goats and sheep.

59. AO 11298   Light buff. 48×34×16 mm. Account
                of goats and sheep. Plate XIII.

60. AO 11299 Light buff. 44×34×17 mm. Pointed
            forms of numbers in front of (mu).
            Text unfinished.

61. AO 11300 Light buff. 46×34×14 mm. Account
            of goatskins, goats, and sheep.

62. AO 11301 Gray-buff. 41×32×14 mm. Pointed
            forms of numbers. Account of
            threshed barley.

63. AO 11302 Light buff. 47×33×16 mm. Account
            of goatskins and sheepskins.

64. AO 11303 Buff to gray. 66×45×21 mm. A
            parallel text in AO 11308. Memo
            concerning various commodities de-
            posited with one person. Plate XIV.

65. AO 11304 Buff to gray. 44×33×20 mm. Note
            concerning the purchase of a house.
            Plate XIV.

66. AO 11305 Gray. 59×37×17 mm. Account of
            threshed barley.

67. AO 11306 Gray. 44×32×15 mm. Account of
            threshed barley, emmer and wheat.

68. AO 11307 Light buff. 50×36×15 mm. Witnessed
            memo concerning two amounts of silver
            deposited by two persons with one
            person. Plate XIV.

69. AO 11308 Light buff. 68×48×19 mm. A parallel
            text in AO 11303. Memo concerning

various commodities deposited with
one person. Plate XV.

70. AO 11309   Buff-gray. 58×40×18 mm. Witnessed
memo concerning the issue of oil and
grain as provisions for a person.
Plate XVI.

71. AO 11310   Buff-gray. 64×40×18 mm. Memo concerning four items (two objects,
silver, a sheep) and a loan. Plate XV.

72. AO 11311   Buff-gray. 67×38×17 mm. Pointed
forms of numbers. Account of threshed
barley and emmer.

73. AO 11312   Gray. 69×36×15 mm. Memo concerning
the deposition of silver and barley
with one person. Plate XVII.

74. AO 11313   Buff-gray. 80×46×18 mm. Pointed
forms of numbers. Account of
threshed barley.

75. AO 11314   Light buff. 68×55×24 mm. Pointed
forms of numbers in lines 9 and 15.
Account of sheep and goats.

76. AO 11315   Light buff. 66×60×17 mm. Two-column
text. Account of sheep and goats.

77. AO 11316   Gray-black. 75×48×21 mm. Witnessed
contract concerning the purchase of a
person. Plate XVIII.

78. AO 11317   Gray-black. 66×42×20 mm. Witnessed

contract concerning the purchase of
a person. Plate XIX.

79. AO 11318   Light buff. 50×34×18 mm. Pointed
                 forms of numbers. Account of goats,
                 sheep and goatskins.

80. AO 11319   Buff-gray. 51×41×20 mm. Witnessed
                 contract concerning the purchase of
                 a person. Plate XX.

81. AO 11320   Buff-gray; originally brown, parts
                 became gray after fire. 64×50×24 mm.
                 Witnessed contract concerning the
                 purchase of a person. Plate XVII.

82. AO 11321   Light buff. 30×27×15 mm. Pointed
                 forms of numbers. Account of goats.

83. AO 11322   Light buff. 28×24×15 mm. Account of
                 goatskins.

84. AO 11323   Gray-buff. 25×23×17 mm. Account of
                 sheepskins.

85. AO 11324   Gray. 20×17×12 mm. Pointed forms
                 of numbers. Account of threshed
                 barley.

86. AO 11325   Gray. 27×23×16 mm. Account of barley.

87. AO 11326   Light buff. 25×24×16 mm. Account of
                 unusual kinds of goats.

88. AO 11327   Light buff. 25×20×15 mm. Account of
                 one sheepskin.

89. AO 11328   Light buff. 28×22×14 mm. Account
              of sheep and goats.

90. AO 11329   Gray. 28×26×14 mm. Account of
              threshed barley.

91. AO 11330   Gray. 27×24×13 mm. Pointed forms
              of numbers. Account of threshed
              barley.

92. AO 11331   Light buff. 31×26×14 mm. Account
              of one goatskin.

93. AO 11332   Buff-gray. 27×22×14 mm. Account of
              goatskins.

94. AO 11333   Light buff. 32×27×14 mm. Account
              of goats and sheep.

95. AO 11334   Light buff. 32×27×14 mm. Account
              of one goatskin.

96. AO 11335   Light buff. 23×22×13 mm. Account
              of one goatskin.

97. AO 11336   Light buff. 25×23×12 mm. Account
              of threshed barley, emmer and wheat.

98. AO 11337   Light buff. 26×22×13 mm. Account
              of one sheep. Plate XVIII.

99. AO 11338   Light buff. 25×22×14 mm. Account
              of one sheepskin.

100. AO 11339   Light buff. 28×23×14 mm. Account
               of goatskins.

101. AO 11340   Light buff. 27×25×13 mm. Issue of
               barley.

102. AO 11341   Light buff. 25×23×14 mm. Account
                of one goatskin.

103. AO 11342   Gray. 28×25×14 mm. Account of
                threshed barley.

104. AO 11343   Gray. 28×26×14 mm. Receipt of
                barley and emmer.

105. AO 11344   Gray. 30×24×14 mm. Memo concerning
                grain placed in two storehouses.

106. AO 11345   Light buff. 27×24×13 mm. Account
                of three sheep.

107. AO 11346   Light buff. 29×26×13 mm. Account
                of two goats.

108. AO 11347   Gray. 32×27×16 mm. Account of
                threshed barley.

109. AO 11348   Light buff. 26×25×13 mm. Account
                of one goatskin.

110. AO 11349   Gray. 22×20×11 mm. Account of
                (threshed) emmer.

111. AO 11350   Light buff. 32×25×13 mm. Account
                of sheepskins and goatskins.

112. AO 11351   Dark gray. 27×25×13 mm. Account of
                threshed barley and emmer.

113. AO 11352   Light buff. 30×27×14 mm. Account
                of goatskins.

114. AO 11353   Buff-gray. 29×23×15 mm. Account of
                one goatskin.

115. AO 11354   Light buff. 30×25×14 mm. Account
                  of threshed barley.

116. AO 11355   Light buff. 26×22×13 mm. Account
                  of goats, sheepskins and goatskins.

117. AO 11356   Light gray. 28×25×13 mm. Account
                  of threshed barley.

118. AO 11357   Light buff. 24×22×12 mm. Account
                  of one goatskin.

119. AO 11358   Light buff. 29×23×14 mm. Account
                  of sheep and goats.

120. AO 11359   Light gray. 30×26×13 mm. Account
                  of threshed barley.

121. AO 11360   Light gray. 32×25×14 mm. Account
                  of threshed barley.

122. AO 11361   Light buff. 27×23×13 mm. Account
                  of one goatskin.

123. AO 11362   Light buff. 36×28×15 mm. Account
                  of one goatskin and of one sheep.

124. AO 11363   Light buff. 36×28×14 mm. Witnessed
                  memo concerning the deposition of
                  silver with a person. Plate XIX.

125. AO 11364   Buff. 29×26×13 mm. Receipt of
                  barley.

126. AO 11365   Light buff. 28×23×13 mm. Account
                  of three goatskins.

127. AO 11366   Light buff. 25×24×12 mm. Account

of one sheepskin.

128. AO 11367   Light buff. 27×26×13 mm. Account
                 of sheepskins.

129. AO 11368   Dark gray. In two small fragments;
                 nothing recognizable.

130. AO 11369   Light buff. 28×25×13 mm. Some forms
                 of numbers are pointed; cf. AO 11402.
                 Signs without meaning. Probably a
                 school exercise.

131. AO 11370   Gray. 32×28×14 mm. Pointed forms
                 of numbers. Account of onions.

132. AO 11371   Light buff to gray. 55×40×17 mm.
                 Context unrecognizable.

133. AO 11372   Light buff. 35×30×13 mm. Pointed
                 forms of numbers. Account of goats
                 and sheep.

134. AO 11373   Gray. 49×37×16 mm. Account of
                 copper objects.

135. AO 11374   Light buff. 43×30×15 mm. Account
                 of sheep.

136. AO 11375   Light buff to gray. 33×28×14 mm.
                 Account of threshed barley, emmer
                 and wheat.

137. AO 11376   Light buff. 37×33×16 mm. Account
                 of five goats.

138. AO 11377   Light buff. 42×28×17 mm. Pointed
                 forms of numbers. Account of sheep

and goats.

139. AO 11378   Light buff. 45×32×13 mm. Account
of goatskins.

140. AO 11379   Gray. 44×34×19 mm. Account of
barley.

141. AO 11380   Light buff. 40×32×15 mm. Account
of one goatskin.

142. AO 11381   Light gray. 37×31×15 mm. Pointed
forms of numbers. Account of
threshed barley and emmer. Plate XX.

143. AO 11382   Light buff. 40×32×15 mm. Account
of wheat and emmer.

144. AO 11383   Gray to black. 35×28×16 mm. Account
of threshed barley.

145. AO 11384   Light buff. 42×33×15 mm. Account
of threshed barley.

146. AO 11385   Light buff. 63×41×19 mm. Account
of sheep and goats.

147. AO 11386   Light buff-gray. 44×33×17 mm.
Poihted forms of numbers. Account
of goats.

148. AO 11387   Light buff-gray. 54×37×18 mm.
Pointed forms of numbers. Account
of sheep and goats.

149. AO 11388   Light buff. 67×42×17 mm. Account
of fields.

150. AO 11389   Buff-gray to black. 60×46×20 mm.

Witnessed contract concerning the
purchase of a person. Plate XXI.

151. AO 11390   Buff to gray. 66×44×20 mm. Witnessed
contract concerning the purchase of a
field. Plate XX.

152. AO 11391   Buff. 68×58×21 mm. Witnessed contract concerning the purchase of a
field. Plate XXII.

153. AO 11392   Reddish buff. 59×60×22 mm. Witnessed
contract concerning the purchase of a
field. Plate XXIII.

154. AO 11394   Gray. 66×37×18 mm. Pointed forms
of numbers. Account of fields.

155. AO 11395   Gray. 52×39×19 mm. Witnessed contract concerning the purchase of a
field. Plate XXIV.

156. AO 11396   Light buff. 52×36×16 mm. Account
of sheep and goats. Plate XXI.

157. AO 11397   Light buff to gray. 45×32×15 mm.
List of five persons.

158. AO 11398   Buff to black. Top destroyed. 44×
47×18 mm. Witnessed contract con-
cerning the purchase of a person?
Plate XXII.

159. AO 11399   Light buff. 45×32×15 mm. Account
of goatskins and goats.

160. AO 11400   Violet/red tinge on brown background.

55×43×20 mm. List of names of
workers?

161. AO 11402   Buff to gray. 47×38×17 mm. Some
forms of numbers are round, others
pointed. Cf. AO 11369. While all
signs are clear, the meaning of the
text is not understandable.

162. AO 11403   Light buff. 36×27×14 mm. Account
of linen garments.

163. AO 11404   Buff-gray. 42×34×16 mm. Pointed
forms of numbers. Cf. also AO 11405
and 11409. Size of a field. Plate
XXIII.

164. AO 11405   Buff-gray. 47×36×17 mm. Text very
badly preserved; apparently similar
to AO 11404 and 11409.

165. AO 11406   Buff-gray. 38×35×17 mm. Pointed
forms of numbers. Account of
garments.

166. AO 11409   Light buff to gray. 52×40×16 mm.
Pointed forms of numbers. Cf. also
AO 11404 and 11405. Size of a
field. Plate XXIII.

167. AO 11410   Light buff. 68×40×17 mm. Pointed
forms of numbers. Account of
workers.

168. AO 11411   Gray. 72×42×20 mm. Contents not
understandable. Plate XXIV.

169. AO 11412   Gray to black.   94×46×25 mm.
                Witnessed contract concerning the
                purchase of two fields.   Plate XXV.

170. AO 11413   Light buff.   Perforated cone, 60 mm.
                high and 40 mm. in diameter.   Witnessed
                memo concerning an oath? taken by one
                person.   Plate XXV.

PLATES

PLATE I

1. (AO 7983)

2. (AO 8636)

3. (AO 8637)

4. (AO 8638)

PLATE II

5. (AO 8639)

7. (AO 8641)

6. (AO 8640)

8. (AO 8642)

PLATE III

9. (AO 8643)

15. (AO 11131)

PLATE IV

10. (AO 8959)

11. (AO 8960)

PLATE V

17. (AO 11255)

14. (AO 11130)

PLATE VI

16. (AO 11254)

PLATE VII

19. (AO 11257)

11262

24. (AO 11262)

PLATE VIII

33. (AO 11271) 27. (AO 11265)

PLATE IX

31. (AO 11269)

32. (AO 11270)

36. (AO 11274)

PLATE X

37. (AO 11275)

39. (AO 11278)

41. (AO 11280)

PLATE XI

47. (AO 11286)

40. (AO 11279)

PLATE XII

50. (AO 11289)

44. (AO 11283)

PLATE XIII

51. (AO 11290)

56. (AO 11295)

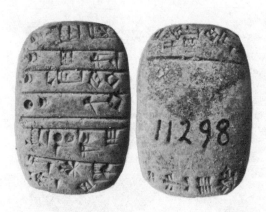

59. (AO 11298)

PLATE XIV

64. (AO 11303)   65. (AO 11304)

68. (AO 11307)

PLATE XV

71. (AO 11310)

69. (AO 11308)

PLATE XVI

70. (AO 11309)

PLATE XVII

73. (AO 11312)

81. (AO 11320)

PLATE XVIII

77. (AO 11316)

98. (AO 11337)

PLATE XIX

78. (AO 11317)

124. (AO 11363)

PLATE XX

80. (AO 11319)

142. (AO 11381)

151. (AO 11390)

PLATE XXI

156. (AO 11396)

150. (AO 11389)

PLATE XXII

152. (AO 11391)

158. (AO 11398)

PLATE XXIII

153. (AO 11392)

166. (AO 11409)

163. (AO 11404)

PLATE XXIV

155. (AO 11395)

168. (AO 11411)

PLATE XXV

170. (AO 11413)

169. (AO 11412)